THE TRUE WILDERNESS

The true wilderness

BY

H. A. WILLIAMS

CROSSROAD · NEW YORK

1982
The Crossroad Publishing Company
575 Lexington Avenue
New York, NY 10022

Printed in the United States of America

Library of Congress Catalog Card Number: 81-70889

ISBN 0-8245-0470-4

ACKNOWLEDGMENTS

I should like to thank Messrs A. R. Mowbray for allowing me
to include here 'The True Wilderness', originally published in
Lenten Counsellors. I also thank the following for permission
to quote from their works: Mr John Betjeman and Messrs
John Murray for 'In a Bath Teashop' (on page 106), from
Collected Poems by John Betjeman; Mr T. S. Eliot and
Messrs Faber and Faber for twelve lines (on pages 20, 38 and
108) from *Four Quartets;* Mr W. H. Auden and Messrs Faber
and Faber for six lines (on pages 91 and 103) from 'In Memory
of Sigmund Freud' from *Collected Shorter Poems;* and
Messrs Duckworth for four lines (on page 71) from *Ladies and
Gentlemen* by H. Belloc.

H.A.W.

CONTENTS

Introduction

Most of the sermons collected here were delivered in the Chapel of Trinity College, Cambridge. It will be obvious that they are in no sense an attempt to expound a systematic theology. Nor do they represent the views of any particular theological school. People better qualified than myself have expounded the thought of Barth and Bultmann and Tillich and Bonhoeffer, and the value of the expositions in provoking thought has been shown by the controversies they have started. The aim of the writings collected here is more modest, and their character more personal.

Part of my work has been concerned with preparing men for the Theological Tripos in Cambridge University. This work of teaching consists in expounding the Old and New Testaments and the early Church fathers as they are understood in the light of contemporary scholarship. Such an academic study of basic Christian writings is an essential preliminary to the understanding of Christian truth. But more and more it has been borne in upon me that, however essential, such study is no more than a preliminary. For the knowledge so acquired remains always external to the self, like a house one owns and inspects regularly and the details of which one can draw up accurately for an estate agent but which one has never lived in nor made into a home. Academic theology is as essential for a knowledge of

Christian truth as a house is to a home. But only if it becomes part of what I am, like my home, can it be the living truth which Christ came to give. Christian truth, in other words, must be in the blood as well as in the brain. If it is only in the brain, it is without life and powerless to save, as much a parody of itself as Mr Gradgrind's definition of a horse. Nobody denies that a horse is a quadruped, graminivorous, with forty teeth, and the rest. But the description not only conveys nothing of the living animal but gives the impression that horses are the invention of pedants. So it is, I believe, with those accounts of the Christian faith served up solely by the brain for the brain.

I decided, therefore, that alongside of teaching academic theology I would try to ask myself how far and in what way a doctrine of the creed or a saying of Christ had become part of what I am. The pulpit seemed the obvious place from which to expound what I thus discovered. And I resolved that I would not preach about any aspect of Christian belief unless it had become part of my own life-blood. For I realized that the Christian truth I tried to proclaim would speak to those who listened only to the degree in which it was an expression of my own identity. Previously, it seemed to me, I had often been like a man who, while perhaps he enjoyed a good tune, was essentially unmusical and who attempted from the books he had read to describe the quality of Beethoven's quartets. And I wondered how much I had thereby contributed to the emptying of the Churches by making the Christian gospel appear unreal and irrelevant to people's lives.

I said I decided on this course. But that is misleading. The decision was taken for me in some area of my being over which I had no control. I found it became impossible to propound an official point of view like a political speaker taking a party line. Such a procedure appeared so false to myself that the words would not come. Unless what I proposed to say came from the depths of my own experience, I was struck dumb. By some people this was interpreted as the loss of one set of beliefs and the adoption of another, as though I had used my liberty as an Anglican to reject the doctrines of Catholic orthodoxy in favour of some more modernistic creed. But this has not in fact been the case. I found it equally impossible to expound Tillich or Bultmann from the pulpit as Thomas Aquinas or Charles Gore. And although I have been psycho-analysed and have read many of the works of Freud and Jung, learning a great deal from them, I could not propagate their opinions like a new gospel based on a fundamentalist acceptance of what they wrote. What was withheld from me was the ability to transmit second-hand convictions whatever their source, orthodox, modernist, or non-Christian. All I could speak of were those things which I had proved true in my own experience by living them and thus knowing them at first hand. It may comfort some people to label this procedure existentialism. But although I have read Heidegger and Sartre, I am not aware of being one of their disciples. What I have been forced to attempt is something different – to describe only those places where I myself have lived and belonged. There is nothing unusual about it. The same thing is done by every genuine artist in any medium. And had it not been done by St Paul and St John, not to mention Christ Himself, there would be no Christianity at all.

The result is not so much intellectually unsatisfactory as intellectually unsatisfying. The intellect craves for complete systems of explanation set out with logical coherence. What we owe to such systems, in the realm, for instance, of natural science, is too obvious to need enlarging upon. Civilization itself depends upon the capacity of the intellect to systematize its experience. But there are areas of human life where explanatory systems can falsify as well as illuminate. Personal relations are an obvious example. The dogmas of this or the other school of psychology may well illuminate the profound feelings which two people have for each other, but only up to a point. When that point is passed and the claim is made that a human relationship can be reduced, without remainder, to the terms of a psychological explanation, the explanatory system falsifies to absurdity. If we want further illumination we turn from the textbook of psychology to the work of the novelist and the poet. Here we find a point of view certainly, a general outlook on life. But it lacks the mathematical completeness and the neat coherence of an abstract theory and leaves us with all sorts of loose ends. For the novelist and the poet, if they know their job, are not constructing theorems. They are trying to give expression to life as they have known it in their own experience, mysterious, many-coloured and often inconsistent.

What is true of personal relations is *a fortiori* true of man's relationship with God. Systems of explanation illuminate up to a point and then falsify. And when the attempt is made to gather up the totality of man's experience of God within the confines of some systematic orthodoxy, then the falsification can be considerable. What is being described here is not intellectual error. The theological definitions provided may be true in their own sphere, like Mr Gradgrind's definition of a horse or the descriptions of human motivation in the text-book of psychology. It is that the wine of life cannot be contained within the bottles of intellectual definition and if we stick to the bottles, failing to perceive that they have been burst by the wine, then we find ourselves with no wine. An example of this has been provided by recent discussions about the God out there. For many people the concept of the God out there is a burst and empty bottle. That is not to deny that it has contained wine and still contains it for a lot of people. Nor is it to claim that the new bottle suggested, God as the depth of my own being, will not itself be burst and broken when it has served its turn. The discarding of the old bottle and the provision of the new has been interpreted by some Christians as a denial that there is any wine at all. That is because they have imagined that God can be contained within the limits of a definition as though wireless waves were identical with a certain type of receiving set. Yet the fact that God cannot be thus contained or identified was for St Paul part of the scandal of the cross. The Greeks, he said, seek after wisdom; yet the world by its wisdom failed to find God, who is known not in intellectually satisfying systems of thought but in the muddle and agony of a man being executed.

It is true that Christian thinkers have attempted to systematize the teaching of Christ. But the success of the endeavour depends upon seeing some things which are not there and not seeing others which are. If we can imagine that the teaching had just been discovered and that a hostile critic was bent on denigrating it, it is not hard to see what a field-day such a critic would have in exposing the obscurities and inconsistencies in the sayings recorded. For Christ spoke from immediate

11

experience and what He gave in His teaching was Himself and not any rounded theory of God and man. 'We testify what we have seen.' The use of the plural in this saying indicates that Christ is speaking not only of Himself but also of His disciples. Unless they, too, testify what they have seen, their witness will be dead, however perfectly it fits any yardstick of doctrinal orthodoxy. And it is to this task that I believe myself to have been called. The result will be found in what follows in this book. It may have a message for some. It will certainly say nothing to many. But at least it is not an exercise in theorizing.

If, however, there is no attempt at systematization in the following pages, there are certain themes which tend to recur and on which the sermons look like a number of variations. This has not been a matter of deliberate policy. The themes appear to have chosen me rather than I them in the sense that they are the issues with which, without my choice, I have been most deeply involved. The most often recurring is death and resurrection, the necessity of dying to various forms of superficial life if one is to have life abundant. Closely associated with this theme is that of riches as Christ spoke of them – not necessarily material wealth but anything to which we cling in order to preserve superficial and ultimately bogus life and hence to evade the frightening necessity of dying and being born again to our true selves. Human life is very largely a wilderness, a dry land where no water is. Riches are the artificial grass and plastic flowers with which we try to cover up the stony ground and persuade ourselves that we live in a watered garden. Death is the realistic acceptance of our wilderness for what it is, a refusal to cover it up with simulated appearances of life. Once we thus accept

our wilderness and no longer try to hide it from ourselves, there follows the miracle of resurrection. The
desert becomes verdant. The stony ground itself brings
forth rich pastures. It is, for instance, the man who faces
and accepts his inability to love who discovers within
himself a power of loving which nothing external can
destroy or diminish. And this is life through death.

The experience of death and its attempted evasion
and of resurrection to true riches undreamt of before,
although I believe it to be the very core and essence of
the Christian gospel, has not been set out in markedly
religious language. This is not because I have decided
that mankind has come of age and therefore needs
religionless Christianity, but because, on examination,
my own deepest experiences seem to be profoundly
human, belonging to man as man and not simply to
people who are religious by temperament or training.
I am aware that for a long time, without knowing it,
I used my religion as an attempted escape from the
ambiguities and anxieties which belong inevitably to
being human in contradiction to the basic Christian
belief that God took the fullness of humanity upon
Himself. Indeed a great deal of Christian prayer and
endeavour seems to be founded upon an implied dualism
(however much intellectually Christians believe in one
God) and issues in the hope that the Redeemer will
save us from a Creator who has endowed us with
instincts and desires of which we are afraid. I have
discussed this in my Hulsean Sermon, and the theme
emerges more than once in the following pages.

The New Testament speaks of God sending His Holy
Spirit to dwell within us and of Christ in us the hope
of glory. Must we not therefore look for God in what
we are, in the whole kaleidoscope of our personal

experience? And in this sense would it be wrong to speak of a theology of the self? These sermons are an attempt at such a theology. The decision to publish them has of course been deliberate. But in the writing of them I had no choice. I could do no other.

Trinity College
Cambridge

Into all truth

St John 16 : 13 – *When he, the Spirit of truth, is come, he will guide you into all truth.*

Nowhere in the New Testament do we find words more terrifying than these. Perhaps you think it strange that they should be called that. Obviously some people fear the truth – bigots, reactionaries, obscurantists of one sort or another – but not us with our liberal education and open minds. If Cambridge has done for us what it's meant to do, then surely we, of all people, can welcome with serenity and pleasure our Saviour's promise that His Spirit will guide us into all the truth.

There are, however, two kinds of truth which I'm going to call the outside kind and the inside. Universities are concerned only with the outside kind of truth. They train us to observe objects or ideas as accurately as possible and to see as fully as possible how these objects or ideas are related to each other. From us, as people, what we study keeps its distance. It's a sort of mental money – worrying only if you haven't got any; otherwise our property, over which we have complete control. So we speak of the expert as somebody who has mastered the subject. And where there is mastery, there is no sense or risk or feeling of danger. The facts are his. Once they have been assimilated, he exercises dominion over them as a rational being.

But the inside kind of truth can never be mastered in this way. I have called it inside because it doesn't keep its distance from us. It has a life of its own and can therefore sweep in upon us in ways we can't control. Take, for instance, something of superlative beauty – music, painting, what you will. We can indeed study and master its outside truth – how it is constructed and how related to what has gone before and so forth. But its reality eludes us altogether unless it penetrates us and evokes from us a response we can't help giving. In this sense, far from being in control, we are ourselves mastered by what we see. The same of course is true of what repels and terrifies us. We speak of being haunted by it – ugliness, brutality, meanness. We look the other way. We try not to think of it. We won't read that sort of novel or see that sort of film. And thereby we confess the power which these things can exercise over us. Or take our relations with other people. In any society our relations with most of its members has to be largely impersonal. Without this impersonality, life would be utterly impossible. If each of us were deeply involved with everybody else, the place would be a lunatic asylum. For other people can remain the outside kind of truth so long as we know them only superficially. We can master the art of dealing with them – what is called social *savoir-faire*. But once we know them at all well, the relation is no longer completely under our control. They have a certain power over us, whether we want them to or not. When I say, 'So and so gets on my nerves,' it means that my relation to him has become the inside kind of truth.

This sort of truth is always hitting out at me in one way or another. It conjures up something within me

16

previously dormant – love, hatred, happiness, misery, fear, anger, peace, joy. It never leaves me as I was. Always it brings a blessing or a curse. And both are really me, aspects of myself generally submerged and unenfranchised, now raised to the surface and given a voice in what I am.

But extending the franchise always seems a risky business, and there is bound to be considerable opposition. And so the temptation is strong to treat the inside kind of truth as though it were the outside kind. We call it, naturally enough, something rather grand – being objective. But in these circumstances, objectivity is a funk-hole. It is an attempt to keep at arm's length realities which I fear will evoke me too painfully by making me meet sides of myself I prefer to ignore.

According to St Paul, this is what people do with God. 'The world,' he said, 'through its wisdom knew not God.' Paul was not an anti-intellectual. The point he is making is that God can never be the outside kind of truth, the conclusion of a philosophical or scientific investigation. For a cool head and a cold heart never yet led any man to know any sort of love, least of all the love which passes knowledge. Such theological objectivity is an attempt to keep God out, because His love will confront us with our full selves, and we all have our skeletons in the cupboard. This is what led Kierkegaard to say, 'the theologian is the anti-Christ.' Yet it need not be so. For all the really creative theologians of the Church, St Paul, St John, Augustine, Luther, Pascal, or our own Westcott – all of them realized that theological truth can never be a matter of juggling with ideas, however brilliantly. All understood that it must be found inside them or not at all.

17

'Thou mastering me, God' – that is the ultimate truth.

'When he, the Spirit of truth, is come, he will guide you into all truth.' Not by means of scientific discovery, or logical argument, or some masterpiece of intellection, but by evoking the me I've always refused to meet and enabling me to take this despised and rejected person fully to myself, breaking down the middle wall of partition. And the Holy Spirit does this within me, by means of my own character and my own experience, by means of what I am. 'We are not,' said Von Hügel, 'to think of the Holy Spirit, and the human Spirit, God and the soul, as two separate entities. God's spirit works in closest association with ours.' Or in the words of St Catherine of Genoa (the creator of modern hospital work), 'My me is God, nor do I know my selfhood save in Him.' When people say, 'Not me, not me, but God, God over there,' they are trying, whether they know it or not, to escape from ultimate truth because they feel it will be too much for them. They objectify God in order to keep themselves at a safe distance. But when the Holy Spirit leads us into all truth, He will be, as Christ said, within us, not outside; within the whole of us, and not just in the Sunday-best part of us – the times when we feel pious and decent or pure in heart. For, as far as we are concerned, the chief work of the Holy Spirit is to reconcile what I think I am with what I really am, what I think I believe with what I really feel; to liberate what fear compels me to suffocate, to introduce the me I loathe and fear and cut dead, to introduce this very me to the glorious liberty of the children of God.

Consider one of the practical consequences of this. I go to the Holy Communion and experience God's love and beauty. Afterwards I find myself in a worse

temper than usual or more full of desire. It probably
worries me, yet this is exactly what I should expect.
My communion with God has given me the confidence
to accept a little more of what I am. The prayer in the
hymn has been answered – 'What is frozen, warmly
tend'. And it is only by being thus first unfrozen, that
these potentialities of mine can be afterwards trans-
formed to contribute to goodness and love. Keep them
permanently in quarantine, and they will always remain
my enemies – and God's.

But this makes Christ's promise very terrifying. Instruments I kept locked in a drawer have now been
put into my hands, ultimately so that I can use them to
create beauty and all things good. But until I've learnt
how to use them, I feel much worse off than I was before, more discontented, more restless, more anti religion
in its established form, more anti convention, the Spirit
of Christ bringing me not peace but a sword. It's
unavoidable. If what the collect calls our unruly wills
and affections must be not liquidated, but made
available – for only so can they be ordered aright – then
I'm bound to be in for a stormy time. Most of us often
refuse to allow ourselves thus to be made available. I
believe that, so long as we refuse in this way, we are
committing the sin against the Holy Spirit which cuts us
off from the abundant life Christ promised us. It's like
the talent which, for fear, the man hid in the ground.

And please notice one further thing. Because the
Holy Spirit is within us, because He can be known only
subjectively, only, that is, by means of what I am, we
shall never feel absolutely certain that it is in fact the
Spirit who is working. This is the price which has to
be paid for inspiration of every kind. Is it all nonsense,
after all? I suppose that's why an artist or writer is so

sensitive about the reception of his work. If the critics tear it to pieces, they echo his own inevitable doubts of its validity. And that's why we too can get so hot under the collar when we are judged by conventional standards. For it is our predicament never to be able to escape the question, is it the Holy Spirit or is it Beelzebub the Prince of the devils? Did not Christ Himself, as He was dying, cry out, 'My God, my God, why hast thou forsaken me?' (For faith consists in the acceptance of doubt, not, as we generally think, in its repression.) And must not this show that He was facing the most terrible of all possibilities – that His critics had been right after all? But if faith fails, this inescapable doubt – our human predicament – will drive us into the funk-hole of objectivity, what the Bible says, what the Church says, what they, whoever they are, tell us to believe and to do; they, the orthodox experts – who crucified Jesus because He trusted the Spirit within Him and not the establishment. It is right that on Whit Sunday we should offer thanks to God and praise His holy name for sending us the Spirit of His Son. But let us not be blind to how much the gift will cost us. It is a dreadful thing to be guided into all truth. 'Are ye able to be baptized with the baptism that I am baptized withal?' Yet only thus can we ever be satisfied or learn what living means. 'The dove descending breaks the air With flame of incandescent terror.' But this fire only threatens and hurts. It never injures. Still less does it consume. On the contrary, by this fire alone can we have life and have it more abundantly. For

> Love is the unfamiliar Name
> Behind the hands that wove
> The intolerable shirt of flame
> Which human power cannot remove.

What does it profit a man?

St Luke 9 : 25 – *What does it profit a man if he gains the whole world and loses or forfeits himself?*

People try to lose or forfeit themselves in a great variety of ways. It is the most comprehensive and the most persistent of all the temptations which beset our human frailty. And if this loss or forfeit of ourselves can assume forms which most Christians condemn as evil it can also assume forms which many Christians inconsistently applaud as wholly good.

But let us proceed by way of example.

We will start with the most effective preacher in this or perhaps in any other century, Adolf Hitler. To millions his message came as the power of God unto salvation. And what was his message? To forget oneself, to lose oneself, in order to find a new identity in the Fatherland. The general outline of this message (as distinct from the particulars) is of course one of the commonplaces of pulpit oratory, and, properly handled, it seldom fails to exercise a strong appeal. For in a disguised form it offers us an escape from the burden and the danger of being ourselves.

This fact goes far to explain a success even greater because more widespread than Hitler's – the success of

21

Communism in the world today. The communist system does not lap its devotees into an economic Utopia. For the mass of the people life remains as hard as it ever was. But Communism does offer this immense spiritual appeal – 'Not I, but the Party which dwelleth in me.' An enormous release of energy is thus made possible. Delivered from the responsibility of being myself, I can mobilize all my vitality in the service of the sacred cause. My very slavery brings me a new sense of freedom.

But there are other ways in which people try to lose or forfeit themselves. Let us, by way of contrast, take the worldling, the man described by St John as living for 'the lust of the flesh, the lust of the eyes, and the empty pomp of life'. This man, too, is seeking an escape from himself. It sounds paradoxical, because from one point of view he is the most selfish man imaginable. But examine his selfishness more closely. As sensuality it shows us a man who is afraid of his latent powers of love and heroism, a man who says to himself, 'Not I, with my capacity to give myself away. That may land me God knows where. Not I, therefore, but a certain amount of physical pleasure which expresses nothing beyond itself.' As boasting and conceit his selfishness shows us a man who is afraid he isn't there, and who therefore says to the world, 'Not I, but my money, my class, my family, my friends, my career, my position, my reputation.' It is the attitude of somebody who denies all value to his own being and points at things external to himself, shouting, 'That, that is me.'

But the worldling is not the only person who tries thus to deny himself. At the other end of the scale, there is the person who is persistently and self-consciously occupied in good works – shall we say a good woman

22

in the worst sense of the word? She has decided to drown her own troubles by helping others. Inevitably the recipients of this altruism find her a trifle exhausting. That is because she has nothing to give. All she can give is herself – and her very activity is an attempt to escape from herself. Fugitives need shelter. They cannot bestow it. And forgetting her own troubles in the service of others is in fact a euphemism for flight.

But there is a cleverer way of laying aside the dangerous burden of our own selves. And here the engine of escape is our intellect. If I can explain a thing rationally, then it is possible for me to feel that I have disposed of it. I have, shall we say, a nightmare in which hell is let loose and I wake up in a cold sweat. But I think I can explain it. It is all due to the cheese *soufflé* I had for dinner the previous evening. What a relief. I need not face up to myself. The explanation enables me to avoid the depths of my own being. This is called being objective about ourselves. In reality, it is a masterpiece of evasion. Of course, if we are at all intelligent we are not satisfied with any gastronomic explanation of ourselves. We are capable of greater subtlety than that. We can put our personality under a microscope, divide it up into this and that complex, this and that inhibition, this and that maladjustment, and there we are spread out in little pieces upon the table. We have explained ourselves away and we have all the freedom of the deserter. The same result can be obtained the other way round. It is obvious that the intellect cannot solve the riddle of our existence. What we are defies explanation. Then let us get on with what we are doing and not worry about the rest. By hard work, fresh air, and exercise, we can at least prevent ourselves having waking dreams.

Clearly, in most men and women there is this urge to evade the responsibility of being the mysterious, dissatisfied, potentially dangerous, and potentially magnificent people they are. It is too much like carrying a ton of bricks and playing with fire at the same time. Why not therefore lose or forfeit oneself?

Now it is fatally easy for the Christian propagandist to exploit this tendency, and thus to play the part of the devil masquerading as an angel of light. 'You say you are weary and frightened or perhaps just dissatisfied. You want to escape from it all? Well, some people try escape by embracing a political ideology, others by living for pleasure, others by identifying themselves with some superior set or class, others by enveloping the man in some form of professional success, others by good works, others by explaining themselves away, others by not thinking. But Christianity offers you a much more successful escape than any of these.'

'Observe. I am a Catholic priest, and as such the spokesman of a church infallible in matters of faith and morals. And thus I can tell you what you are and where you are going to and why. I can fit you in to a cosy universe, like a ship into a bottle; telling you what to believe and how to behave. We have mapped it all out long ago. All you have to do is to deny yourself, to resign your proud independence of judgement, to submit in humility to Holy Church which will look after you like a mother her child.' Of course, that is not the whole story. For one thing Rome insists that the most important fact about any and every man is his capacity for goodness – in theological language, that the image of God in man is not obliterated by original sin. And this has often given men courage to be themselves. For another thing, Rome has canonized people – a St Teresa

24

of Avila, a St John of the Cross – who have not been content with the cosy universe of the standard map, but who, always alone and often in great travail, have explored the mysterious heights and depths of their own being and have found in such self-knowledge and self-acceptance a peace which passes all understanding. Yet the other side remains – the appeal to abandon the responsibility of independence for the protective arms of mother church.

But if Rome has exploited this ultimate form of human cowardice, the Protestants have exploited it infinitely more. Take, for instance, Calvin's doctrine of predestination. It destroys human responsibility altogether, dividing men and women into two classes – those who are and those who are not the happy prize-winners in God's own lottery. As with its Marxist or Communist counterpart, such determinism undoubtedly gives people a new sense of freedom and releases an enormous amount of energy. The moral, and indeed the commercial, vigour of communities believing in predestination has been notorious. Yet even for gaining the whole world the price of losing one's own soul is too great. But the issue, in its religious form, is no longer a living one. Much more important is the Protestant doctrine that man comes into this world incapable of goodness, that the image of God in man, as Luther taught, is completely destroyed, that, as our own Article 13 says, works done before the grace of Christ are not pleasant to God and have the nature of sin. This doctrine reverberates through the prayers we still pray, and the hymns we still sing. 'There is no health in us.' 'Just as I am without one plea.' 'Nothing in my hands I bring.' 'I am all unrighteousness.'

Now the appeal of this doctrine, that in ourselves

we lack all value and are incapable of goodness, the appeal of this doctrine is extremely strong. It tugs at us with considerable force. But it is the same old temptation we have been considering throughout in a religious disguise. It is another form of that comprehensive appeal to lose or forfeit ourselves, to play the deserter, to escape from the effort and the danger of being the man I am. I am not yet perfect. I have not yet fully found myself. My desire always exceeds my performance, and this is liable to produce a sterile and torturing anger. On the other hand, I am afraid of my potentialities. They may lead me into any sort of hell or high water. I am tired as well as frightened. The road seems endless as well as dark. Then, give up, capitulate, show the white flag. Admit that you haven't found yourself because there is nothing to find. Admit that you are weary because you go on pretending that you have value when in fact you haven't any value at all. Find your peace by denying yourself absolutely, by confessing that you are a mass of corruption – 'There is no health in me' – your complete and utter unworthiness, by losing your identity in order to find a new one outside yourself. It feels very much safer.

But, as Christians, we must remember that it was not by coming *down* from the cross that Christ entered into His glory. His *death* was the greatest of all acts of self-affirmation. Against everything exterior, against the world, He held to the truth that was in Him. He held to the truth which was Himself. It was no clear prefabricated vision. He had to find it. He had to find Himself. In Gethsemane, we are told, He began to be greatly amazed and sore troubled. On the cross, as the earliest evangelist did not shrink from telling us, He felt the torture of despair. He allowed Himself to feel

26

this supreme pain of despair rather than to jettison Himself in some act of self-abrogation. He cried, 'My God, why hast thou forsaken me?' He did *not* cry, 'My God, I have always been wrong about everything. Receive me on the basis of this admission.' By thus refusing to forfeit Himself whatever the cost, He was able to say, 'Be of good cheer; I have overcome the world.'

There are short cuts to peace of a sort and to freedom of a sort. We have only to sell the one pearl of great price which often seems so much more of a liability than an asset. But there are no short cuts to glory. There are no short cuts to that perfect self-knowledge and self-fulfilment which possesses all authority in heaven and on earth. And it is for such glory that we were made – that is what we fumblingly affirm when we say that Christ rose from the dead.

Often we shall have to change the direction of our thinking and our wishing and our striving. That is what repentance really means – taking our bearings afresh and trying a new road. Often we shall have to allow the dynamite of life to smash up those fixed attitudes of heart and mind which lead us to make demands in their nature self-contradictory. In this sense we shall have often to lose our life in order to find it. To take an example from something which effects us all most intimately, we all have to discover for ourselves – and it can be in agony – that possessiveness never leads to possession, and that it is only the generosity which makes no demands that elicits the full-hearted satisfying response. And for this we have first to learn to love ourselves, because, without such generous love of self, our love for others, whatever its outward manifestations, becomes in its inner essence a compulsive grasping in

27

which we try to compensate from their personality for the value which we deny to our own.

No, it can be no easy journey, this voyage of discovery in which we set out to find ourselves. The road to the celestial city is a long road. In places it must needs be stony and steep. And as we travel we shall not always be certain of arriving at our destination. Yet from time to time we shall ascend the Delectable Mountains, and from there we shall behold the city from afar, perceiving something of the breadth and length and height and depth of what is to be fully ourselves. In such fleeting moments of vision we reckon that the sufferings of this present time are not worthy to be compared to the glory which even now is being revealed in us. And this it is which gives us hope, and makes us count them happy which endure.

The true wilderness

It is a pity that we think of Lent as a time when we try
to make ourselves uncomfortable in some fiddling but
irritating way. And it's more than a pity, it's a tragic
disaster, that we also think of it as a time to indulge in
the secret and destructive pleasure of doing a good
orthodox grovel to a pseudo-Lord, the pharisee in each
of us we call God and who despises the rest of what we
are.

But this evening I don't want to speak about the
disguised self-idolatry which will be practised in our
churches on Ash Wednesday. For Lent is supposed to
be the time when we think of Jesus in the wilderness.
And the wilderness belongs to us. It is always lurking
somewhere as part of our experience, and there are
times when it seems pretty near the whole of it. I'm not
thinking now of people being ostracized, or without
friends, or misunderstood, or banished in this way or
that from some community or other. Objectively, as a
matter of actual fact, these things happen to very few
of us. Most people's wilderness is inside them, not outside. Thinking of it as outside is generally a trick we
play upon ourselves – a trick to hide from us what we
really are, not comfortingly wicked, but incapable, for
the time being, of establishing communion. Our wilderness, then, is an inner isolation. It's an absence of

contact. It's a sense of being alone – boringly alone, or saddeningly alone, or terrifyingly alone. Often we try to relieve it – understandably enough, God knows – by chatter, or gin, or religion, or sex, or possibly a combination of all four. The trouble is that these purple hearts can work their magic only for a very limited time, leaving us after one short hour or two exactly where we were before.

As I said, our isolation is really us – inwardly without sight or hearing or taste or touch. But it doesn't seem like that. Oh no. I ask myself what I am isolated from, and the answer looks agonizingly easy enough. I feel isolated from Betty whom I love desperately and who is just the sort of woman who never could love me. And so to feel love, I think, must be at the same time to feel rejection. Or I feel isolated from the social people who, if noise is the index of happiness, must be very happy indeed on Saturday evenings. Or I feel isolated from the competent people, the success-boys who manage to get themselves into print without getting themselves into court. Or I feel isolated, in some curious way, from my work. I find it dull and uninviting. It's meant – it used – to enliven me and wake me up. Now it deadens me and sends me to sleep. Not, in this case, because I'm lazy, or thinking of tomorrow's trip to London, but because it makes me feel even more alone. Or I feel isolated from things which once enchanted me, the music I play, the poetry I read, the politics I argue about. I go on doing it now as a matter of routine, not in order to be, but in order to forget, to cheat the clock. The L.P. record will take forty minutes if you play both sides, and then it will be time for tea. Or perhaps I've been robbed, robbed of my easy certainties, my unthinking convictions, that this is black and that is white, and Uncle George was a saint, and what they told me to believe is true and the opposite false, and my parents are wonderful people, and God's in his heaven and all's right with the world, and science is the answer to everything, and St Paul was a nice man, and there's nothing like fresh air or reading the Bible for curing depression – fantasies, like children's bricks, out of which I thought I should build my life, and which now have melted into air, into thin air, leaving me with nothing. Out of what bricks, then, I ask in despair, am I to build? Is it to go on always like now, just – tomorrow and tomorrow and tomorrow – a slow procession of dusty greyish events with a lot of forced laughter, committee laughter, cocktail laughter, and streaks of downright pain?

But what I've been describing is the true Lent, the real Lent, which has nothing to do with giving up sugar in your tea, or trying to feel it's wicked to be you. And this Lent, unlike the ecclesiastical charade, this sense of being isolated and therefore unequipped, is a necessary part, or a necessary stage, of our experience as human beings. It therefore found a place in the life of the Son of Man. Because He is us, He too did time in the wilderness. And what happened to Him there shows us what is happening to ourselves. Here, as always, we see in His life the meaning of our own.

What then happened to Jesus in the wilderness?

I believe that in the later gospels the story has been written up. It looks to me like a sermon from an early Christian preacher, one of the greatest sermons ever delivered. But, even so, it can't compare with the stark simplicity of our earliest record. Here it is, and in this case at least St Mark tells us more by being less talkative than St Matthew and St Luke. At His baptism in

31

Jordan, the Spirit of God had descended upon Jesus, and in His heart there rang an immediate certainty of being chosen to do great things – 'And there came a voice from heaven, saying, Thou art my beloved Son, in whom I am well pleased. And immediately the Spirit driveth Him into the wilderness. And He was there in the wilderness forty days, tempted of Satan; and was with the wild beasts; and the angels ministered unto Him.'

If we say this is poetry, we're not saying it's unhistorical, but simply that a bare record of outward events can't convey the truth about man, and so the truth about the Son of Man.

What does the story tell us?

Notice first that it is by the Spirit that Jesus is driven, thrown out is the actual word, into the wilderness, the same Spirit which had brought Him the conviction of being called to do great things. The Spirit is ourselves in the depths of what we are. It is me at the profoundest level of my being, the level at which I can no longer distinguish between what is myself and what is greater than me. So, theologically, the Spirit is called God in me. And it is from this place where God and me mingle indistinguishably that I am thrown out into the wilderness. The story of Jesus reminds us that being thrown out in this way must be an inevitable concomitant of our call to God's service. To feel isolated, to be incapable for the time being of establishing communion, is part of our training. That is because so far our communion has been shallow, mere pirouetting on the surface. We've come to see its superficiality, its unrealness. Hence the feeling of loss. The training doesn't last for ever. In fact, new powers of communion with our world are being built up within us. We are being made the sort of people of whom it can be said, 'All things are yours.' But it belongs to the training to feel it will last for ever.

And so, we are tempted of Satan. Tempted to give up, to despair. Tempted to cynicism. Tempted sometimes to cruelty. Tempted not to help others when we know we can, because, we think, what's the use? Tempted to banish from our life all that we really hold most dear, and that is love, tempted to lock ourselves up, so that when we pass by people feel, 'There goes a dead man.' And behind each and all of these temptations is the temptation to disbelieve in what we are, the temptation to distrust ourselves, to deny that it is the Spirit Himself which beareth witness with our spirit. God in us. The water in the bucket of my soul doesn't look like the ocean. Yet every Sunday we affirm that it is. For in the creed at the Holy Communion we speak of the Spirit as He who with the Father and the Son together is worshipped and glorified. We say it, but every day we're tempted not to believe it. And this self-distrust conjures up the wild beasts. Sometimes they're sheer terror, panic, which makes us feel about the most ordinary undangerous things, 'I can't do it'. Or the wild beasts are the violent rages roaring inside us, triggered off by something ridiculously insignificant – a word, a glance, a failure to show interest in some petty concern. Or the beasts prowl around snarling as envy, hatred, malice, and all uncharitableness.

This then is our Lent, our going with Jesus into the wilderness to be tempted. And we might apply to it some words from the First Epistle of St Peter: 'Beloved, do not be surprised at the fiery ordeal which comes upon you to prove you, as though something strange were happening to you. But rejoice, in so far as you share Christ's sufferings, that you may also rejoice and be glad when his glory is revealed.'

Christ's glory is His full and satisfying communion with all that is. It is the opposite of being isolated. All things are His and He fills all things. This complete communion springs from a love which is able to give to the uttermost, a love which doesn't give in order to get, but which finds in the act of giving itself its own perfect satisfaction. To love is to give. To give is to be. To be is to find yourself in communion with all about you. And this communion is glory. Christ's glory and yours. You don't have to wait for it until you die or the world comes to an end. It can be yours now. Accept your wilderness. From the story of the Son of Man realize what your Lent really means, and then the angels will minister to you as they did to Him. In other words, you'll find moments when giving for love's sake really satisfies you, really makes you feel alive and in contact. And at such moments Christ's glory is revealed, and we rejoice and are glad. We look at the travail of our soul and are satisfied. Lent, we discover, is Easter in disguise.

The relevance of Christ
to psychology

Soon after the war, in the main London stations, posters were put up to which British Railways objected, and eventually, I believe, had removed. The posters were sponsored by some Bible Society or other and consisted in a well-known text from the prophet Amos, 'Prepare to meet thy God.' I want to use that text this morning because it sums up in the best way I can discover the topic about which I am to speak: the relevance of Christ to psychology.

Here let me say at once that by psychology I do not mean experimental psychology – what is done in laboratories to rats and dogs. That work is immensely valuable, but its method of experiment and observation is identical with that of the Natural Sciences, and hence its very proper inclusion as a possible subject in the Natural Sciences Tripos. The relevance of Christ to the study and achievements of science is of course one of the most important of all topics. But I cannot speak of it today, since there would not be time enough even if I were competent to do so. By psychology then I shall mean the analytic methods of depth psychology initiated by Freud and carried on both by disciples and deviationists who, while they may differ in a variety of

35

ways, all agree in affirming the existence of an unconscious as well as of a conscious mind and in believing
that our growth to maturity as persons depends upon a
proper balance in the relation between these two.

How is Christ relevant to psychology so understood?

Well, I suppose one of the most obvious ways is concerned with the truth. You will remember that Jesus
said of Himself, 'I am the truth,' and to His disciples,
'Ye shall know the truth, and the truth shall make you
free.' You may see somebody acting a part on the stage
and wonder what he is like in real life. But in what we
thus call 'real life' people still continue acting, assuming
various roles in the various circumstances of existence
and behaving consistently with them. There is nothing
wrong in this. Indeed, life in any community depends
upon our capacity to play a part in this way. As a
tutor, for instance, I cannot always say to a pupil what
I would say to an old and intimate friend, and sometimes it would be absolutely wrong to do so. Or Mr
Smith conducting political business in the lobbies of
Westminster will not be quite the same person as Mr
Smith in the intimacy of the family circle. The trouble,
however, is that we often confuse what we really are
with these roles which it is our duty to play. We identify
the man with the actor, and in the service of this
identification we disguise our feelings from ourselves.
We imagine that those feelings are appropriate to the
roles we have assumed and think of as us. Let us take
an example. There is such a thing as genuine righteous
indignation. Jesus showed it when He drove the money
changers with whips from the temple. And in my role
as a public-spirited citizen concerned with the common
good, it may be that when confronted with some evil

I too, like Jesus, will feel genuine righteous indignation. But, on the other hand, it may be that what I imagine to be righteous indignation is really something else: rage at my inherent inability to enjoy myself as do those I condemn. In this case, what I think of as righteous indignation is in fact a feeling of impotence, with anger and jealousy resulting. Or again, there are open-minded people dedicated to the pursuit of truth wherever it may lead them. And for the sake of this sacred cause they are prepared to defy any and every authority. Perhaps I am one of those people. But it may not be so. My sense of being on a crusade against the pretentious ignorance of Mr Big may in fact be something I despise so much that I hide it even from myself – an infantile hatred of the first Big I came across (Mrs Big this time), my mother for not loving me when I wanted her to. Psychological investigation, in so far as it succeeds, shows up the sham feelings of which we are the victims and brings us into a realm of truth which sets us free in a very practical way. When feelings are recognized as out of date and as having nothing to do with objective circumstances, then although we may still have them, we shall cease to be their slave. I may still get into a raging temper, but at the same time I shall say to myself, 'Well, that's me,' and I shan't think it's due to some swine or other over there. In this gradual understanding of the truth about ourselves, it is the light of Christ our Creator which is shining in the darkness and enabling us to take a first long step towards that love of our neighbour which He has commanded. Thus it is God we meet whenever we meet something of our true selves, however unpleasant that something may be. In the time of Amos, people were light-hearted and confident at the apparently pleasing prospect of meeting God. They desired the Day of the Lord to come. But Amos knew better: 'Woe unto you,' he said, 'who desire the day of the Lord. For it is darkness and not light.' When we discover something of our real feelings it will often seem more like darkness than light, for our feelings will often not be the good and benevolent ones we thought they were. Yet paradoxically it is in that very darkness that God meets us and the darkness is the beginning of His light. For to see things as they are is to see them as God sees them.

Locked up inside each one of us are some very horrible things – ruthless aggression, for instance, especially in the form of a powerful drive to use sex, not as a means of deep personal encounter, but as an instrument to assert ourselves regardless of other people, to subdue and conquer another person for our own satisfaction. We also find hatred and malice because we cannot feel accepted – primarily by ourselves. And we also find despair – despair in proportion to our incapacity to feel and realize our own value. Before Freud, these things were known to exist, but they were considered to belong only to odd and peculiar people, to a small minority of civilized men. Freud believed, and many would add he demonstrated, that they were the common inheritance of us all, including nice friendly people like you and me. Most of us can keep them hidden from ourselves most of the time, shut off in the unconscious. If so, then the best thing is to leave well alone and not to worry. 'Human kind,' wrote T. S. Eliot, 'Cannot bear very much reality.' Perhaps it is God's plan for many of us that we should wait for purgatory before we begin to be confronted with a great deal of what is inside us. But many others of us are forced to begin confronting it now. We start being aware of the turbulent forces within: the violence, the cruelty, the panic, the utterly self-regarding will to power, the deadness and the despair. Unsolicited, such things may break into consciousness to be felt as though they would take complete possession of us. What depth psychology has shown is that the breaking into consciousness of these unconscious drives is not illness, but a move, often an agonizingly painful move, towards personal integrity, towards our inheriting the fullness of what we are, so that we become real people instead of stereotypes. Or to put it in religious language, when we receive more of what we are it means that for us purgatory has begun. We are being made into what God always intended for us. But how can this be the case if what we receive is violence, hatred, despair and all the other things which are absolutely opposed to God's nature, opposed to love and joy and peace?

But Christians believe that God revealed Himself in Christ. Christ lived in no ivory tower. He took upon Himself, He felt to the full as His very own, the horrifyingly destructive forces which lie latent in us all, so much so, we are told, that at one time his sweat was, as it were, great drops of blood falling down to the ground. When some small element of that turbulent agony becomes your own, then, more than at any other time, you are with Christ and He is in you. You are closest to Him when you feel furthest from Him, just as He was closest to His Father's heart when He cried, 'My God, why hast thou forsaken me?' Our redemption is a mystery. It can only be lived. It cannot be explained.

But when in the violence and horror of your feelings, or in their deadness and despair, you are allowed to enter Gethsemane and find Christ, then you see, perhaps only fitfully, for brief moments, the one miracle worth having: the miracle of transformation, the conversion of destructiveness into life, of soul-destroying hatred into life-giving love, of despair into joy. For by our willingness to receive and feel these immense evils working within us, by that, we are receiving Christ who took all evil into His own heart and used the horror and agony of it to give Himself utterly to His Father, thus bringing good out of evil itself. Perhaps we may say that when a person becomes aware of the dark forces latent in him the result is a feeling of valuelessness which is terrible chiefly because we do not know what to do with it. How can we go on living feeling so utterly without value? But Christ in Gethsemane suggests that this very experience of utter valuelessness is itself of supreme value – man's finest hour, when he is most royal in the exercise of his human prerogative. Certainly it is a fact of Christian experience that when you are with Christ in His bloody sweat, although you will remain there perhaps for a long period, at the same time you will also be reigning with Him in the peace of God which passes all understanding. The prophet's words, 'Prepare to meet thy God,' become no longer a threat. They become a promise that whatever our conscious mind may have to receive from the dark depths below, there God is, mighty to save.

Bonhoeffer, in a well-known remark, complained that the churches were offering cheap grace. I believe that in the same sense the churches sometimes tend to offer cheap therapy, presenting Christ as a sort of psychiatric patent medicine which quickly cures us of our disturbing feelings. I believe this to be theologically wrong. First, God must be loved for what He is in Himself and not as a means on earth of winning heaven or of escaping hell. Secondly, there is no reason to suppose that in any individual at any particular time God is necessarily on the side of the psychic *status quo* any more than in a nation at any particular period He is necessarily on the side of the political or economic *status quo*. Indeed, since we have not yet apprehended and have not yet been made perfect, the opposite is to be expected. And, thirdly, the New Testament everywhere insists that we can know the power of Christ's resurrection only if we also know the fellowship of His sufferings. If, without our choice or contrivance, feelings arise within us which cause distress, then Christ is there in the distress itself, not to save us from the pain of rebirth but to assure us that we are indeed being born again. To change the analogy: when, of old, there stirred in Abraham the desire to leave the city where he belonged and to travel he didn't know where, perhaps the most obvious course would have been to persuade him that he suffered from wanderlust – a disturbance of which God would cure him. And when, after a few months, the cure complete, he settled down contentedly once again in Ur of the Chaldees, you could have talked of Theotherapy. But Abraham would have lost everything – his vocation, his integrity, his soul. He would have been the victim of the cheap grace which is not grace.

The relevance of Christ to psychology cannot be of any real concern to those whom God has not yet called to receive into consciousness the darkness that is within them. But those whose distress reveals that this divine call has come, those people can, in Christ's words, look up and lift up their heads, for their redemption draweth nigh. Like the shepherds at Bethlehem, they will be sore afraid. But to them also comes the message, 'Fear not: for, behold, I bring you good tidings of great joy. Emmanuel. God with us.

Gethsemane

We heard in the lesson this evening St Matthew's account of Jesus in the Garden of Gethsemane. Christians have always believed that Jesus was truly and fully man. He wasn't a god dressed up in the body of a man as though manhood were a suit of clothes. According to St Paul, Jesus emptied Himself of His Godhead. Whatever this means, it means that His experience as a human being was identical with our own. He did not know everything in the past and future. He knew just as much and just as little as we do. Nor, having emptied Himself of His Godhead, could He restore it to Himself as an emergency measure. He had no more power in reserve than the ordinary human person. As the New Testament says, He was in all things like unto us.

In the light of these facts, what happened to Jesus in the Garden of Gethsemane? He was frightened, indeed St Mark says He was panic-stricken. Why? For a variety of reasons. First of all, He was cornered. Any sane man in His position would have known that He could no longer escape the authorities and that the authorities would execute Him. And what had happened to His life-work, His mission? It lay in ruins. One of the twelve disciples had already betrayed Him. The others, he could see, were, like Himself, perplexed, and

43

could not take much more. They would desert Him soon. To the three of them He knew best, He opened something of His heart, trying to tell them a little of what He was going through so that they could share it with Him and support Him with their understanding. But it was too much for them. They could not take it in. They were stupefied. And when He turned to them for reassurance they had found escape from His trouble in sleep. Jesus was left entirely alone with His panic and horror. Even we ourselves in a small way know something of what it is like to be cornered and up against what has become out of our control, how we go over things in our mind, go over and over them again. This will help us to understand a little of what Jesus was thinking in Gethsemane. Had He done the right thing in attacking the authorities so aggressively? If they were now set on killing Him, was not that chiefly His own fault? If He had been more restrained, quieter and more tactful, the authorities would not now be seeking His blood. He might still be teaching the crowds, largely unopposed. And wouldn't that have been better for everybody concerned? Had He not perhaps been too hasty, too violent? Going into the temple and driving out the money-changers and traders with whips – wasn't that suicidally provocative? And if He had been over-emphatic and in too much of a hurry, perhaps that showed that somewhere He wasn't certain of Himself. When He was baptized in the Jordan and struggled with temptation in the wilderness, He had felt supremely confident that He was right. And when the crowds came to listen to His teaching and the sick people He touched were healed, there seemed no shadow of a doubt that He was God's Messiah. But now? The old confidence, the old certainty, had left Him.

44

Perhaps from the start He had been the victim of an illusion. After all, that sort of thing had occurred fairly frequently in the history of His people. They had always had their false prophets as well as their true ones. And many of the false prophets had been sincere enough according to their lights. They had just been a bit mad, that was all. Had He been a bit mad too? And was this the moment of disillusioning sanity? Had He sacrificed everything to a fanatic's dream? After all, His relatives had thought Him mad, and at one point had tried to force Him to come home. And how ruthless He had been with them for the sake of the cause He thought He embodied. He had disowned them when they came to look for Him – His mother, His sisters and brothers, all of them – and He had said that His real mother and sisters and brothers were those who followed Him. Wasn't that to get things out of proportion, evidence perhaps of an insane conceit? Perhaps Judas Iscariot was right and it was best for everybody that He should be arrested and crucified. And Judas, what right had He to bring untold suffering and calamity upon the head of Judas? For that was certain to happen. Judas had a great deal of loyalty in him, a great deal of good. That is why He had chosen Judas to be a special friend. Had He not stretched Judas's loyalty and love, all those good qualities which had made him so obvious a choice, stretched them beyond all human endurance? And so, was not He Himself responsible for His own betrayal by Judas? Judas would feel intolerable remorse, that was certain, and it would lead him to do something desperate. And was not He Himself to blame, even more, much more, than Judas? No wonder Peter, James and John were asleep. He had rebuked them, and talked of watching and

45

praying, but what right had He to demand sympathy on so colossal a scale? Wasn't it best for them that they couldn't give it? Let them sleep on and take their rest. The doubt, the insufferable turmoil, the going over of things in His mind again and again, the agony, were His and His alone. There was nobody to share His desperate uncertainty, the torturing doubts, the terrifying emptiness, the menace from outside of His approaching arrest and execution, and the infinitely worse menace from inside of disillusion and despair.

So it was that Jesus prayed, 'Father, if it be possible, let this cup pass from me.' He was human enough to want to be let off what He was going through, humble and honest enough to admit it. But the simple request from the depths of the heart, 'Let this cup pass from me', was qualified : 'Father, if it be possible.' It is natural and absolutely right that we should not wish to be put too severely to the test. But, having said this, we must add that God is most emphatically not an escape from human ills enabling us to evade the horrors and suffering of human life. Too often in the past, God and religion have been presented as pain-killers, as though God were a magician who will melt our troubles away like snow in the sun, giving us a divine relief from the hard facts of the real world. But God is not a funk-hole, how-ever much Christians may have tried to use Him as one. And this is what Jesus understood when to His natural request for relief He added, 'If it be possible.'

It was not possible. What menaced Jesus from outside and tortured Him from within could not be removed. The betrayer came with the police, the friends of Jesus deserted Him and ran away in a panic. He was duly arrested, sentenced and executed. Nor, as far as we can tell from our earliest record, St Mark, did

46

Jesus find peace or the quiet of certainty. For most of
the time He was silent and had nothing to say. At the
end, just before He died, He cried out, 'My God, My
God, why hast thou forsaken me?'

As with Jesus, so with us, there is no escape from
the human situations in which we find ourselves. God
will not say, 'Abracadabra', and get us out of it. Nor
will He supply us with a spiritual drug to deaden whatever doubt or anxiety or fear or pain may come our
way, and cheer us up so that we feel good. Perhaps we
confuse escape with something quite different: victory.
For Jesus there was no escape. But there was victory.
Yet how, if He died deserted by men and feeling forsaken by God? How victory?

The victory consisted precisely in not running away,
in not trying to escape. In things outside this meant
staying in Jerusalem and facing the worst His enemies
could do. That is obvious. More important, it meant
squarely facing the enemies inside – the doubts, the
despair, the perplexity, the panic, the isolation. From
these enemies inside, Jesus did not hide under a cloak
of illusion, pretending to Himself that things were better
than they were and that He was feeling like a hero. He
accepted His agony – not a glorious uplifting experience,
but an experience powerful to wound and warp and
destroy. He accepted what He thus found within Him.
He knew that there would be no angels to bear Him
up and guard Him from all ills. And by thus facing
and accepting what came to Him from outside and
from within, without lessening the agony, He mastered
it. He made it into His servant. He used it as the way
of surrender, of giving all. The agony of which He
might have been no more than the victim was by
acceptance converted into the instrument of His will.

He had always wanted to give Himself. And when, as now, He was stripped of everything and had nothing to give, by consenting to receive that state of affairs and not hiding away from it, He used it to give Himself totally. That was His victory. That is how He mastered what happened to Him. We shall be celebrating the victory on Easter Day, but it is present already in Gethsemane. Easter turns the light on a situation already present and shows it in its true colours for what it really is. If Jesus was victorious, it was on this night before He died.

And what of us? It is unlikely that we shall ever have to go through an experience as deep and devastating as Christ's own in Gethsemane. But we may sometime approach it, even if only from afar. Somebody we love and on whom we depend may die. Or our material circumstances may unexpectedly change for the worse. Or something we had set our heart on and were working for devotedly may collapse into nothing. Or perhaps already we have discovered that our real enemies are inside us, that we have an unfortunate temperament in this way or that, that we are assertive or quarrelsome or timid or prone to worry and be anxious, vaguely but disturbingly frightened of something – we don't quite know what. Or perhaps we shall be ploughed up, turned inside out by a turbulent, unsatisfied love. If any of these things are true of us, or become true – and examples could be multiplied *ad infinitum* – then God won't provide a magic escape. If we look to Him to do that, we shall feel He has let us down. What God will enable us to do is to face these unpleasant, ugly, disturbing, frightening, sometimes agonizing facts or feelings. To face them without dodging or pretending to ourselves that things are different, and thus to accept them. 'This is me.' 'This is the corner I am in.' 'This is how I feel.' And as with Jesus, so with us, the acceptance will bring the victory. By not evading our circumstances, outside us and inside, we shall cease to be their victim and make them bring us the very life which they would rob us of. I know a man who was blinded in the war. He was invalided out of the army. Life seemed at an end for him. At first he bitterly resented what had happened to him. For a time, his inner turmoil, his anger and hatred and exasperation and despair caused him even more suffering than his blindness. Then gradually he began to accept not only his blindness, but also his immense resentment at it. After about a year, he discovered that he could compose music (although somebody else had to write it down for him). His music has not yet been published. Perhaps it never will be. But that is irrelevant. He wasn't looking for fame or reputation. He was looking for life. And he found it in the music he composes. A few years ago, he said to me, 'You'll think it very odd, but before I was blinded my life was terribly shallow. I sometimes wonder whether I was alive at all. Now I have found a richness and peace which before were unimaginable. Of course, being blind is still hell. But I have learnt to live with it and the privations it brings. And had I not been blinded, I don't think I should ever have discovered the deep happiness I now possess underneath the pain.' This man had been with Jesus in Gethsemane. He had mastered his fate by accepting it. When that happens, we want to thank God, because the evil, which is real and hurts, the evil from which we suffer, is changed, transfigured, into good. The very evil which destroys brings us life and peace and joy. Jesus spoke of His passion and death, all the agony of it, as the cup He had to drink. He gives this cup to us to drink with Him. This means pain, and to drink the cup is to accept the pain. But then we find that the cup is something else as well, which is more important and final: the cup of blessing which is the communion of the blood of Christ. As the hymn puts it,

> And oh what transport of delight
> From thy pure chalice floweth.

The pearl of great price

Matthew 13 : 45 – *The kingdom of heaven is like unto a merchant man, seeking goodly pearls: who, when he had found one pearl of great price, went and sold all that he had, and bought it.*

The merchant did not find the one pearl of great price at the beginning of his career. He must have been in business some time before he eventually discovered it. For, in the first place, he had to accumulate the capital needed to buy it. Had it come his way at the start he would not have had enough goods to sell to realize the fortune required for its purchase. And, secondly, without much experience he might not have been able to recognize its supreme value. The instant understanding of its worth could come only after a long time spent in sorting, comparing and evaluating. Had the merchant refused to trade in lesser pearls, he would never have acquired the one pearl of great price.

Jesus said that the kingdom of heaven was like this merchant man. At the very least this means that the kingdom is not something which can be immediately presented to you on a plate, so that all you have to do is to put it into your pocket and feel good. You will find many devout Christians who have forgotten what

Jesus said and who will present the kingdom of heaven to you in exactly this way. It means, they will tell you, adhesion to a given form of doctrinal orthodoxy. Believe this, that and the other, and there, you've got the kingdom. But you haven't got it. All you've got is an excuse to stop looking for it. You may commend the views you have thus accepted with passionate earnestness and zeal, but these may only show that deep down you are afraid that you have been fobbed off with an artificial pearl. All fanaticism is a strategy to prevent doubt from becoming conscious. And meanwhile the apparent agnostic infidel in the rooms above may in his own manner still be seeking for the kingdom of heaven, while you aren't.

Or, some people will tell you that the kingdom consists in obedience to a traditional system of ethics. Do this and don't do that, and yours is the kingdom. Obedience of this kind often looks like a virtue. In fact, it is always a blasphemy. A blasphemy against oneself. To base and regulate one's life upon other people's rules – even when they call them God's Law – this is blasphemous because it is to choose slavery when you could be free. Freedom involves the discovery by each of us of the law of his own being: how he, as a unique person, can express sincerely and fearlessly what he is. And this discovery can be made only by the courageous acceptance of experience, through suffering and joy, through disillusion and fulfilment. If you are content to be conventional or conventionally unconventional, if you are content to be like somebody else and accept as your own the rules of a given type of person, then you have abandoned looking for the kingdom of heaven.

Or, others will tell you that the kingdom consists in stimulating within yourself a certain type of religious experience which is miscalled conversion. If, they say, you haven't had this particular sort of religious experience, then you are outside the kingdom. The trouble is that when you examine the required experience carefully and deeply, you find that it isn't essentially religious at all. True, in the case we are considering, the required feelings are evoked by symbols long associated with religion. But precisely similar feelings can be evoked by symbols which have no religious associations at all. Think of the comforting warmth, the escape from isolation, the wonderful sense of purpose and mission, evoked in Germany by Adolf Hitler. To the half-blind, like ourselves, it is not always so easy as it seems to distinguish between the kingdom of heaven and the kingdom of hell.

But how then are we to enter into the kingdom of heaven? How can we find the one pearl of great price?

Only thus: by refusing to be satisfied with anything less than what is totally satisfying. I don't mean what *should* satisfy us, but what in fact *does*. You know how all invitations are kind invitations and how at all parties we enjoyed ourselves immensely. That is just a polite convention. We musn't treat any prescription for life with a sort of pious *politesse* trying to persuade ourselves that it satisfies when it doesn't. Of course, there is the old saying that half a loaf is better than no bread – a wise maxim in a number of circumstances. But as a policy for living it is utterly irreligious and, if we follow it, it will exclude us absolutely from the kingdom of heaven. For, without deadening part of us, without doing injury to what God has made, we can never be content with half a loaf. We can never be content with less than total satisfaction.

Consider, for instance, the God you have been

brought up with and sometimes worship and vaguely
serve and perhaps half disbelieve. To be honest, isn't
this God rather like half a loaf? Wouldn't it be true
to say that he satisfies you only in part? If so, you must
spend your time here looking for a better God – you
can look for a better God by reading, by thinking, by
discussion, by the experience of common worship and
private prayer, by living, knocking about and being
knocked about. You won't go down from here with a
whole loaf. But you may go down with the inner
certainty that in the end you will get the whole. And
that's the meaning of faith : it is basing your life on the
conviction that to those who ask it shall be given, that
those who seek shall find, that to those who knock it
shall be opened, however long we have to ask and seek
and knock.

Or take our way of life, what we live for, what we
aim at doing, what we value most. Does that satisfy us?
Or does it leave a void somewhere? I'm afraid that's
the sort of thing we simply can't take on trust. We've
got to find it out for ourselves. Some things seem to
satisfy us fully for a time, and then we gradually discover that they fail to cater for a quite important part
of us. There are times, for instance, when some of us
imagine that we can live simply by every word which
proceedeth out of the mouth of God. And then we learn
that we can't, that we have also to live by bread. The
warm human nature we are tempted to despise because
we share it with all sinners refuses to be ignored.
Or, on the other hand, we may imagine that we can
live by bread alone, that worldly success and gratified
instincts are all we need to satisfy us fully. The bread
may remain new for a time, then it gets stale and
suddenly we realize that it has been turned into a stone.

We look around and find ourselves in a waste land surrounded by heaps of rusty abandoned junk. But don't take this from me or anybody else. For if you don't discover it for yourself, in your heart of hearts you will always envy the people you call worldly or wicked. And envy excludes satisfaction.

And this brings us back to the merchant. We said he had to accumulate the capital he needed to buy the pearl of great price. And it was real solid wealth. We often think we can buy the one pearl with paper-money. We are sincere enough when we add up our paper-pounds. We don't want or intend to deceive ourselves. But it is very easy for us to forget that there is precious little real wealth behind the notes we are counting. Our intentions and acts of will are the paper-money. We resolve to do this, to be that, to give ourselves to the other. We forget that there are large areas of the self where the writ of the will simply doesn't run. I resolve, shall we say, to be loving to everybody. That resolve of mine is the paper-pound I pay for the pearl of great price. I forget that my capacity to love is as yet stunted and immature, and that, in the absence of such real wealth, my resolve is worth very little. And so I expect to obtain the pearl and wonder why I don't. I expect to feel fulfilled and satisfied and all I feel is tired and on edge. What we have to learn is that our real capital accumulates slowly, and often without our noticing it. The earth, as Jesus said, beareth fruit of itself. Theologians would say that we grow as people only through the grace of God. But grace isn't a sort of spiritual petrol. It is the creative quality of life itself – all the things we do, all the things that happen to us, working, arguing, listening, playing, falling in love, all the splendours and the miseries, all the pleasure and the pain – it is thus that our real capital slowly accumulates until in the end we can honour the paper-pound of our resolves with the golden sovereign of our whole selves.

And what about recognizing the pearl of great price? What about the instant understanding of its worth?

Christianity presents us with a man upon a cross, a man whose teaching still has the power to thrill, whatever we believe about him, a man who gave everything away in love for others, even life itself. And it points to this man in his death-agony and says that there, in utter complete self-giving, there alone is what satisfies totally. Most of us have brief moments when we know with absolute certainty that so to give ourselves away in love is the full, perfect satisfaction for which we crave. But such moments do not stay. The Crucified soon passes as in a cloud out of our sight. And we are left only half-believing, left to win the truth for ourselves, by trial and error, by false hopes and shattered illusions, and by joy unspeakable and full of glory.

There is nothing in this world or the next, absolutely nothing, which cannot, and will not, be turned into the valid currency we need to buy the one pearl of great price. That is what is meant when we say that we are redeemed.

They that have riches

Mark 10 : 23 – *And Jesus looked round about,*
and saith unto his disciples, How hardly shall
they that have riches enter into the kingdom
of God! It is easier for a camel to go through
enter into the kingdom of God. . . . With men
the eye of a needle, than for a rich man to
it is impossible, but not with God.

Comfortable words, these, for people like ourselves. I
suppose nobody here would regard himself as a rich
man. News may still come to us of mysterious
millionaires from Greece or Turkey or the United States.
But in England we've changed all that. One of the
most remarkable achievements of our time could perhaps be described as making these famous words of
Christ out of date. If we fail to enter the kingdom of
God, it's not because we're rich.

But maybe we've overlooked something : the simple
fact that Christ was a poet. Take poetry as literal
description, and you'll probably find yourself very wide
of the mark. People once did this to the wretched camel
going through the eye of the needle. The eye of the
needle, we used to be told, was a narrow gate in the
wall of Jerusalem – for which there is no evidence of
any kind. Or camel was really cable – as though that

made it any easier. All right, we'll allow the camel and the needle to be a piece of vivid imagery. But the riches, after all, were solid pudding. The young man in the story had great possessions, and he was told to go and sell them. But it belongs to the poet to see in material fact a concrete symbol for some law of life, some spiritual principle, which can't be directly expressed. It's certain that in the young man's material riches Jesus saw something applicable to all men everywhere, whatever their bank-balance. For if not, why did He hammer the point home to His disciples, who were all as poor as church-mice? The very emphasis of His words shows Him feeling His way towards something He intuitively knew to be of immense importance to everybody. It's interesting to notice how this was recognized by the first Christians. Jesus once said, 'Blessed be ye poor.' Fifty years later, the saying appeared in St Matthew's Gospel as 'Blessed are the poor in spirit'. Who can doubt that the interpretation was correct? For the poet always speaks truths deeper than he knows consciously.

'How hard is it for them that trust in riches to enter into the kingdom of God! . . . With men it is impossible, but not with God.'

Let us leave Palestine now for an art-gallery in Florence or where you will. Most of the visitors are trying frantically to accumulate riches. Clutching the *Guide Bleu* with grim determination, they're attempting to make capital for themselves out of the masterpieces they see. They hope that when they emerge, they will possess so much the more culture, so much the more conversation, so much the more cosmopolitanism. What a relief to find in the Uffizi that the last bay is unexpectedly a bar. For making this sort of money is terribly exhausting work. And the sad joke is that the money is worthless. For the masterpieces by means of which they have inflated their own egos have shown them nothing and told them nothing, have sent them in fact empty away. Because they have treated the art gallery as a sort of aesthetic stockmarket, its real treasure is denied them. Their pitiable, laughable riches have excluded them from the kingdom of God. But there are one or two visitors, a Director, shall we say, of the Fitzwilliam Museum, who haven't come to make cultural money. They have come to look. They've come to allow this or that picture to work its magic upon them. What they enjoy is the picture, and not the picture of themselves looking at the picture. So the picture speaks to them, and tells them what must remain a secret because it can't be communicated. Because their total concern is with what they are looking at, and they are not at all concerned to acquire or retain anything, they come away filled with good things. Their poverty has enabled them to enter into the kingdom of God.

Now say I belong to the first *Guide Bleu*-clutching crowd, how am I to become like the second lot? The trouble is that you cannot do it by trying, for trying makes me even more self-conscious than usual. Trying not to make cultural capital out of what I see is a completely hopeless enterprise. Or in Christ's words, with man it is impossible. But not with God. The ability to forget yourself in the wonder of what you see comes like a miracle, maybe just by holding still, something given, not something achieved. Wait for it, and in time it will be yours.

On from Florence, to Cambridge. What about my work? Am I interested in it for its own sake, or am I interested in getting a good class in the Tripos? Well, of course, the answer is both. And let it be said at once that a certain amount of ambition is natural, healthy, and good. Please don't think I'm playing the dishonest trick of trying to make you feel guilty for wanting what all the dons already have. But it remains true that what we study fulfils us, makes us more ourselves, nourishes us as people, opens the kingdom of God, only in so far as we are concerned with its own inherent value, and unconcerned with any riches of prestige we may collect on the way. For a man's life, said Jesus, does not consist in the abundance of the things which he possesses, and that includes Tripos classes.

The same principle is true with regard to the people we know and the people we love. Nothing on earth brings us so wonderfully to our human inheritance, or opens so wide the gates of the kingdom of God, as other people. But this is always on condition that I don't try to make capital for myself out of them. If what I want is to belong to the right set or to be known as the man with the pretty girl-friend, then my friends and my lovers don't bring me more abundant life. Kicks now and then perhaps, but always persistent anxiety about ceasing to count with them, of losing my shares in them.

But the most destructive riches of all are religious riches. How prone we are to trust in them. Perhaps it is our sound attitude towards the Bible, or towards the Church of England, or towards drink. Or perhaps it is our superior sense of emancipation which leads us to despise others as St Paul despised Jewish Christianity. Sometimes our religious riches may consist in a whipped-up sense of sin – to have really succeeded in making myself feel there is no health in me – it's like having a million dollars. Or those warm feelings when we pray –

valid as God's gift when they come unsought, kingdom-shutting riches when we pray in order to have them and won't pray unless we do.

You will see that Jesus was talking about relying for true wealth upon what leaves you bankrupt. A possible word for it would be acquisitiveness or cupidity. I've tried to give you four examples of how in practice this acquisitiveness or cupidity works, and spoils everything. And you can't, I said, cure yourself of it by trying. For this only makes me more than usually greedy for an ungreedy me, and the result is like the ghastly unselfishness of the self-centred, which is infinitely harder to put with than any honest selfishness.

But with God all things are possible. What I believe happens is that we slowly become aware of the game we're playing, and as slowly become convinced that it isn't worth the candle. What therefore we need is not a stronger will, but a deeper insight, not more strength but more light. When, with our total being we begin to realize that riches are the one thing which prevent us from being rich, we shall no longer hanker after them. Such insight we must trust living to bring us, and that not in a day, nor without bewilderment and pain. For it is the whole gospel of gaining our life by losing it, of death and resurrection.

Whoever seeks to save his life

Luke 17:33 – *Whoever seeks to save his life will lose it; and whoever loses it will save it, and live.*

What do these words of Jesus mean in practice?

Their meaning must have seemed obvious enough to the Christians of the first century – the time when the New Testament was being written. Not that there was systematic persecution by the state. Some Christians were martyred in certain places at certain times. But for most Christians such persecution was a potential threat rather than an actual danger. The state did not persecute systematically until a hundred years later. So, for most Christians of this earliest period, losing life did not in practice mean being killed. But what it did mean to all Christians everywhere was losing the sense of belonging, and the sense of belonging is a vitally important part of life. It contributes to a person's identity and gives him a home, a context in which to live. Many of the first Christians were Jews, and in most of the big cities of the Roman Empire there was a considerable and thriving Jewish colony – a closely-knit community with a common religion, common laws and customs, and an intimate social life – a group whose right to live and worship as it pleased was recognized by the Roman Government. To lose one's place in this deep communal life with its long history and sacred traditions must have left a Christian feeling very isolated.

The same must have been true of the convert from paganism. In the ancient world, social and religious life were inextricably interwoven. Religion was not thought of as a private matter – the city to which you belonged worshipped as a whole. So, for instance, in St Paul's day Ephesus was described by its town-clerk as corporately the temple-sweeper or devotee of the Great Diana. And suppose the neighbours next door invited you to supper – at the meal, libations would be offered to the gods, and if you were there it would be next to impossible not to participate in the ceremony. Imagine today a person who thought blood-sports wicked cooped up in a house-party assembled for shooting, and you can get some idea of what it meant to be a Christian in a pagan society. You were a complete outsider and the nagging need to belong must at times have been extremely painful. The first Christians were content to lose all that social side of living because they were convinced that in the Christian gospel, in the love and service of Christ, they had found something incomparably better. That was the sense in which they lost their life in order to live.

Well, you may think, a little bit of history never did anybody any harm, but our circumstances today are totally different from those of converted Jews or pagans in the first century A.D. Here in Cambridge we can join fully in every sort of communal activity without having to subscribe to any form of creed or having to join in any religious ceremony. There is no need for us to lose our sense of belonging, whatever we are – Christians, Atheists, or Hindus. So perhaps we don't have to lose our life in order to live. Perhaps Christ's words are not addressed to people in our situation.

But society – the city, the home, the school, the college, the university, however, we divide it up – society is not only an external reality, something outside us over there. Society is also inside us and part of what we are. We have been fashioned and moulded by it. A child often inherits some of the physical features of its parents. 'Ah,' says the friend of the family, 'you've got your mother's eyes.' In the same way we inherit or absorb a great deal of the mental outlook and emotional attitudes of the society into which we are born. We look at things through eyes, partly at least, already conditioned for us. We see and feel things in ways partly pre-determined. This is society inside us. And it is by means of this society inside us that we feel we belong. It is by means of this common stamp that we are aware of our membership one to another. We don't feel isolated because we share much of our inner thoughts and feelings with those around us. The external city to which we belong is built in miniature within the individual heart and mind.

A curious and sometimes amusing consequence follows. The society outside us to which we belong may be extremely tolerant. Cambridge is, for instance. At the same time, the society inside us may be intolerant to an extreme degree. That is the sort of situation which makes a man into a rebel without a cause. His life is one long protest against apparently nothing – since there is nothing in the external order he wishes to change. What he is up against, without knowing it, is the

64

intolerant tyrant inside. I remember, a year or two ago, having a television discussion with a very militant agnostic lady. Throughout I was at pains to emphasize what happened to be the case – that I was very much in the dark and certain about nothing. However, at the end, the good lady looked at me severely and said, 'You people might sometimes admit you don't know everything.' Clearly she was not addressing the actual clergyman sitting opposite her in the studio. She was addressing a built-in clergyman which was a part of herself.

But towards this built-in city or society we are by no means necessarily hostile. Far from it. More often we regard this internal realm with enormous respect which sometimes merges into worship. And even if we are hostile, our very hostility is a sign that another part of us cherishes and values what we must therefore all the more emphatically condemn. (That is why tirades against sin generally reveal what the speaker most fancies.) Yes, the city inside us is an object of compelling awe. How could it be otherwise? That city was built because we had to belong to a world. In our earliest days we shouldn't have survived at all unless we belonged to a world which would feed and look after us. And since man is by nature social, we still need a society to belong to. No wonder, therefore, that the city outside makes such a deep a lasting mark within us. No wonder we feel we must guard this internal citadel. No wonder we endue it with the value of life itself. No wonder that, for its better protection, we often identify the city inside with truth and goodness. If we want to be polite we call it our inherited convictions; if we want to be rude we call it our inherited prejudices; if we want to be eloquent we call it the great tradition we have been born to serve; if we want to be religious we call it the will of God. But no matter what we call this society within us, and however much from time to time we may want to kick this or that aspect of it, fundamentally we feel with fear and with passion that its preservation is a matter of life and death.

'Whoever seeks to save his life,' said Jesus, 'will lose it; and whoever loses it will save it, and live.' You have come to the university not first of all to equip yourself technically for a job. You have come here first of all to lose your life and save it and live. If this place does for you what it should, you will knock up against all sorts of people with different views about the most fundamental things. You will think and talk and argue and laugh. You will enjoy yourself, but you will also sometimes suffer. For in the general atmosphere of thought and discussion and criticism and laughter, the city inside you may well be invaded and overthrown. What you have so far considered obviously true or false may now seem not so obvious. What so far has appeared as certainly good or bad may now seem not so certain. If by temperament you are an establishment man, certain features of the establishment may begin to look shabby or dishonest. If by temperament you are an anti-establishment man, certain features of your rebellion may begin to look childish and silly. All in all, you will be releasing your grip upon what so far you have lived by, in order that it may be weighed in the balance and its real worth discovered. This invasion and exposure of the city within is, from one point of view, exciting. But it is also painfully disconcerting, since it leaves us for the time being without a world. We find ourselves strangers walking along an unknown path, instead of respected inhabitants of a familiar town. It

feels as if we don't belong anywhere, and we are therefore not unlike the first Christian converts losing the
warm life of their Jewish or pagan past. And now, as
then, the cost of this renunciation is too great for many
people. They seek to save their life by the blind
acceptance of an official orthodoxy – not because after
examination and trial they have found the orthodoxy
true but because it gives them immediate protection,
like a mother's arms, and saves them from the danger
of standing on their own feet. But by thus seeking to
save their life they really lose it. They stagnate
spiritually, shut up tight against the questions life poses
and the demands it makes, making the observances of
their particular orthodoxy into a substitute for living.
Inevitably they become intolerant, telling us that at
all costs we must believe what they say because it is
really God speaking. Fundamentally they are frightened
people, and what they are afraid of is the life which
destroys before it animates.

But what of those others who are willing to lose their
life and live? those who are brave enough to have their
cosy but confined city destroyed in order to find another
which is without limit in the grandeur of its majesty?
At times they will find themselves in the desert. At other
times they will find themselves in pastures more green
than they have ever known before. They will be looking
for a city which hath foundations whose builder and
maker is God. Their journey to the City of God may
bring them to worship in this chapel or it may lead them
away from it. But in either case, whether they are
present here or absent, what they are doing will be shown
forth and lived through Sunday by Sunday. For on every
Sunday morning in this place bread is broken and wine
poured out in remembrance of one who did not seek

67

to save His life, but lost it and is alive for evermore. He is mankind, and His cross and His glory belong to us. As by unfamiliar paths we journey to the unknown and find ourselves renewed by that bracing atmosphere, with Him we shall be dying and rising from the dead.

A kingdom divided

'If,' said Jesus, 'a kingdom is divided against itself, that kingdom cannot stand. And if a house is divided against itself, that house will not be able to stand.' At first glance these words may seem a little trite, a rather platitudinous comment, shall we say, on the state of the Congo? However, they probably don't appear quite so obvious in Africa as they do in England. We're lucky here. In the course of a long history we've learnt a great deal as a nation, and one of the most important things we've learnt is to live together more or less amicably. But we can't take it lazily for granted that this state of affairs will continue without our active co-operation. If each section of our society pursues its own selfish aims (in the matter, for instance, of profits or wages) and disregards the common good, then we shall become a kingdom divided against itself, and it will be the end of England. We're not anywhere near there yet, but it could happen. As Jesus told His disciples, 'What I say to you, I say to all : Watch.'

But in the statement of Jesus with which we started, He wasn't in fact talking about public issues; what we call politics and economics. He was talking about human personality. He had been accused by His enemies of doing an obviously good thing – making a madman sane – by the power of evil. And His reply was that evil can't destroy evil and thus produce good. Of course, nowadays we don't generally speak in such violent terms as people once did. We're much more mealy-mouthed. But the charge that good is being produced by evil means is often being half-expressed. There is, for instance, in many quarters a deep suspicion of psychiatry and psycho-analysis, especially among clerics. Yet these modern techniques do manifestly enable people to live fuller, happier, and more useful lives. And the way in which they are sometimes regarded as somehow unhealthy is a flat contradiction of the principle Jesus here lays down. If good is done, then there is the spirit of God and not the spirit of evil, for a house divided against itself cannot stand. It is a pity that a great number of professing Christians are too frightened to admit this.

And frightened is an absolutely key word. If you want to discover the difference which Jesus made to mankind, and go to the New Testament to find out, the answer given is the casting out of people's lives of fear. Fear, in the New Testament, is considered to be the root of all evil. It is fear which makes men selfish, it is fear which makes them hate, it is fear which makes them blind, it is fear which makes them mad. Fear casts out love, as love casts out fear. Which of the two therefore am I going to choose?

It may well be that in this matter I am a house divided against itself. For instance, yesterday I behaved unselfishly. I stood down in the interests of somebody else. But this hasn't brought me any happiness or peace. My unselfishness wasn't recognized, and I feel angry, miserable, and on edge. Why? Because I was unselfish through fear – fear of being thought selfish and thus losing other people's good opinion. And, probably, mixed up with this, a more subtle and less identifiable fear that somehow things would go wrong with me if I had acted selfishly. No wonder, therefore, that I feel all prickles with regard to the other chap who doesn't share my inhibitions, isn't at all afraid of being selfish, and has thus, at my expense, pushed himself to the centre of the stage without caring a damn. How can I help envying him like hell? You remember the woman in Belloc's rhyme—

> Though unbelieving as a beast,
> She didn't worry in the least,
> But drank as hard as she was able,
> And sang and danced upon the table.

And she makes poor frightened little me feel very wretched with envy. For I have tried to be good by means of an evil thing: fear.

But suppose I have behaved unselfishly out of love? Suppose I knew with deep certainty that I could only be my full self by giving, and that this is what love means. Then yesterday, when I acted unselfishly, I should not have been denying myself, not in the least. On the contrary, I should have been affirming myself. I should have been mobilizing all I am in order to be fully me. And today I should feel happy and at peace, because I should not be a house divided against itself. The self-assertive go-getter for whom I stood down could not in the least exploit my unselfishness. Nobody on earth could. For it would simply have been me being myself. And that would be the end of it. This is the omnipotent strength which comes from a house not divided against itself.

Now, I don't think for one moment that I can summon up this strength by simple will-power. The

71

very idea of will-power implies division – two things pushing each other in opposite directions. What I need I must be given, and that is more light, deeper perception, a less clouded vision of what life is about. How am I to get it? Only in the ancient school of experience, by trial and error, by pain and joy, and, most of all, by faith, a confidence that, in spite of all appearances to the contrary, life is on my side and not against me. This is the confidence which Jesus brought to men. It was summed up by St Paul in ten words, 'If God be for us, who can be against us?' When I begin to be convinced of that fact, I shall begin to be a house not divided against itself.

The first and the last

When words of Jesus are being discussed, something which Christians have always believed is often forgotten: that Jesus was truly and fully human, that he spoke as a man, understood as a man, thought as a man. Now among men there are, by and large, two kinds of understanding. One is analytic, concerned to dissect what it observes and arrange such material with mathematical accuracy into exact patterns. That is how philosophers work – and their logic was taken over by the scientists. There is no need in this space age to commend the virtues of this kind of understanding. Its achievements have been staggering and they include the ability to blow up the world. But there are important areas where the analytic mind is powerless. When, for instance, two people love each other deeply their experience cannot be reduced to a precise intellectual formula without being absurdly caricatured. Here, the analytic has to give way to the second kind of understanding – the intuitive, the understanding of the poet. The truth experienced by the poet cannot be stated in precise terms. Nor can we treat what he tells us as a literal description of reality. The poet uses images, analogies, pictures, in the hope that they will communicate what he wants to say by evoking within his readers an immediate assent, what is often called ringing a bell inside us.

It is clear from the teaching of Jesus that His understanding was of the second intuitive kind. He speaks with the depth of a poet, not with the precision of a philosopher. When therefore He is reported as saying, 'Many that are first shall be last and the last first', this is not to be taken as literal information about the next world, that there will be an order of precedence with first and last places and that we can't tell for certain whether we shall be at the top of the list or at the bottom. Indeed it was this anxious concern for place and precedence which Jesus satirized in a pharisee's dining-room when He advised people to take the lowest seat if they wanted to be moved up higher.

But if the statement that the first shall be last and the last first is not to be taken as literal information, it has none the less an important meaning. In fact it summarizes something absolutely central in the teaching of Jesus, expounded in many ways and by means of a variety of examples : that real life is not to be measured in terms of what a man has been able to accumulate, whether it be possessions, achievements, or personal characteristics. If you consider these things as providing a certain index of what you really are, then you may have to revise your ideas radically and find your estimate turned upside down, with your first as last and your last as first.

But Jesus did not talk in abstractions of this kind. He talked in terms of particular examples. And it is to these therefore that we must turn.

He could, let us be honest, be extremely offensive. And what we may well consider to be one of the more unfortunate examples He gave of the First shall be Last principle was concerned with prostitutes. He said they would enter the kingdom of God before the good

74

religious people of the day. We can well understand how some of those who heard Him thought that such irresponsible talk would lead many people into sin. And indeed we shall misunderstand what He meant unless we set it within a wider survey of His teaching.

There was for instance the rich young man. He was rich in a double sense. Not only did he have many possessions (and wealth was considered among the Jews of those days a certain sign of God's approval and blessing), but he was also morally rich. He had kept all the commandments from his youth up. Yet when he was confronted with the challenge of a lifetime, 'Sell all that thou hast . . . and come, follow me,' he was un-equal to it and went away sorrowful, prompting from Jesus the famous comment, 'How hardly shall they that have riches enter into the kingdom of God!' Compare this upright and valuable member of society – and in the uninhibited pages of the gospel we are told that Jesus, looking upon him, loved him – with another man in the gospels who was a scoundrel and a thief. He certainly had not kept all the commandments from his youth up, but, recognizing that he had no riches of any kind on which to rely, he made a simple request: 'Lord, remember me when thou comest into thy kingdom,' and the answer came immediately: 'Verily I say unto thee, today shalt thou be with me in paradise.' A con-demned criminal was the first to enter into the kingdom of God.

Only an extreme cynic would suggest that there was much in common between criminals and children. But the thief's entry into the kingdom reminds us of Jesus saying that 'except ye become as little children ye shall in no wise enter into the kingdom of God'. Children are not innocent creatures, as Freud, Henry James and

75

Ronald Searle have shown us in their own ways. What is true of children is that they have no riches. They cannot trust to the character they have built up over the years. They cannot say to themselves, 'I am this sort of person. I am not that sort of person.' Hence they are very open to influence. To receive is for them the most natural thing in the world. For the average child life is one long act of receiving. They have as yet no defences against life. When Jesus urged men to repent, He was urging them to become as little children. He wasn't asking them to eat the dust. He was confronting them with the necessity of a radical change of outlook, a fundamental re-orientation of their lives, so that they would no longer trust for security in the persona they had built up – the drama of being me which I continuously stage for my own benefit – so that they would no longer trust that, but have the courage to become as receptive as little children, with all the openness to life, the taking down of the shutters and the throwing away of the armour which that entails. Without such repentance we cannot believe in the gospel, for the gospel announces that our only security is God's love for us, and if we look for security in what we have achieved we cannot find security in what is given us. Try to secure a place high up on the list and you don't appear on it at all.

One of the more scandalous of the stories Jesus told was about work and wages. Some of a man's employees had worked the whole day. Others had worked for only an hour. But they all got the same amount in their pay-packets. Inevitably there were complaints. The object of the story was to focus attention on the generous goodwill of the employer. All must be content to receive what the employer chose to give. The amount of work done was irrelevant. What mattered was the employer's generosity. Jesus seems to have taken over this story from one told by the rabbis of His time. In the two stories everything goes exactly the same until the end. In the rabbis' story the complaint arises, 'we have worked the whole day, and this man only two hours and yet he also has received his whole pay.' The answer is given, 'This man has wrought more in two hours than you in the whole day.' The disruptive twist which Jesus gives to the story in its final stage illustrates why He came to be so disliked and distrusted by the establishment. Yet He wasn't talking about economics or wages-policy. He was forcing home once again the truth that men, in the last resort, can depend only on what they receive. It is the willingness and ability to receive which converts the last into the first.

But the most moving example Jesus gave of this truth is the story of the prodigal son, or better, of the two sons. The eldest must be described as a good son. He respected his father's wishes, stayed at home, ran the family business, and positively oozed with virtue. His status with his father was completely assured: 'Son, thou art ever with me, and all that I have is thine.' But he got the reason for this assurance wrong. It was in fact because he was his father's son. He thought it was because of his exemplary conduct. So his confidence was severely shaken when his scape-grace younger brother returned home and all the loving joyful fuss was made about it. You can understand how the elder brother felt. I mean, where were you, what was the point of all your loyalty and obedience, if the disloyal, selfish, heartless younger brother was treated like a hero? What then rose to the surface and became horribly obvious was that underneath the elder brother's

loyalty and apparent goodness, there lay a deep, smould-
ering hatred of his father. And the fuss over the
prodigal's return fanned it into flame. When the elder
son was angry and wouldn't go in to the party, his
father came out and pleaded with him, and was told,
'You know how I have slaved for you all these years;
I never once disobeyed your orders; and you never gave
me so much as a kid for a feast with my friends.' The
elder brother looked for something earned, for the wages
which are paid in families under one euphemism or
another. He looked for something earned and was confronted with something spontaneously given for the
sheer joy of it. And his moral universe was undermined.

With regard to the younger son, the prodigal, it is
interesting to notice what has been made of him by
religious people. While in fact he is an example of true
repentance – the radical change of outlook, the decision
to base his life on other foundations than those of
pleasure-seeking – he is often used to exemplify the
grovelling, eat-the-dirt act with which repentance is
confused. For the prodigal's real repentance was his
return home. It is often made to appear as if it consisted
in the little prepared set-speech he composed in advance
for his father : 'I have sinned against heaven, and before
thee, and am no more worthy to be called thy son : make
me as one of thy hired servants,' a very prim and proper
little speech which sounds like something composed by
the elder brother. Now although the prodigal went
home with this set-speech in his hand and did in fact
just have time to read it out, in the event it was totally
irrelevant and need not have been said. For we read
of the prodigal, 'But when he was yet a great way off,
his father saw him, and had compassion, and ran, and
fell on his neck, and kissed him' – before the boy could

say anything at all. He then recites his piece, but the father does not reply. He doesn't even listen, so busy is he giving instructions to the servants: 'Bring forth the best robe, and put it on him; and put a ring on his hand, and shoes on his feet: and bring hither the fatted calf, and kill it and let us eat, and be merry.' The prodigal was thus given no opportunity of dwelling on his wickedness or harping on the fact that he wanted to be treated like a menial. For that would have been for him to seek security in his own poor estimate of himself (as if it were a form of riches) rather than in his father's irrepressible love. And when the time came, he found that all that was suitable to the occasion, all that the situation allowed, all he could do, was to receive.

'Blessed are the poor in spirit,' said Jesus, 'for theirs is the kingdom of heaven.' The elder brother's riches, his bitter claim that he had behaved well, were the poverty which excluded him from life. He was the first become the last. The prodigal's poverty, his growing awareness that all he could do was to receive what was offered, gave him everything. He was the last become the first.

What then are we ourselves to do: to accumulate riches or to receive them? Now, we can't decide to do one or the other as we can decide whether to eat our dinner tonight or not. The ability to receive comes slowly and mysteriously, and is itself something given. But if we find life disappointing or dull or difficult or frightening, if somewhere we feel that life is not being all it could be, we can ask ourselves, 'Am I organized to accumulate or to receive?' It is the most important question we shall ever have to answer.

The root of repentance

It's obvious how important repentance is for the Christian. It was part of the basic message of Jesus. He began His ministry by telling men to repent and believe in the gospel. Unless, therefore, we are willing to repent, we cannot be His disciples. Unfortunately, however, words get twisted out of the straight when they are used for a long time. They begin by meaning one thing and come to mean another. Take the word 'prevent' for instance. It used to mean 'to go before'. Now it means 'to stop something happening'. The word 'repentance' has suffered in the same way. It has become saturated with ideas and feelings which were absent from it as used by Jesus. So perhaps I ought to begin by saying what repentance doesn't mean. It doesn't mean feeling guilty. Guilt is a form of self-hatred. And hatred never does any good and always does harm, especially when it is my hatred of me. The trouble with a great number of Christians is precisely that they feel guilty about being themselves. This saps their vitality and makes them less effective people than the apparently non-religious. Let us therefore be clear that to repent does not mean to feel guilty. Sometimes people think it means trying to make yourself sorry for the things you have done in the past. Yesterday, shall we say, I went to a party, got rather drunk and kissed all the girls. It was really great fun, and I still feel that it was. But today I'm trying to make myself sorry about it. The trouble with repentance in this sense is that I'm not really being honest with myself. Most of what I am still approves of what I did, and this makes my attempted sorrow ridiculously artificial. Or perhaps I did something which brought unpleasant consequences: I neglected my work, quarrelled with the boss, and lost my job. I'm now involved in the tedious business of trying to get another which won't be so good. In common parlance I'm repenting at leisure of my laziness and bad temper. But it isn't repentance as Jesus used the word. When I experience the unpleasant consequences of doing certain things, my resolve not to do them again is a matter of mere instinct. The man who won't eat oysters because they always make him ill can hardly be described as an example of repentance.

But if the word doesn't mean feeling guilty, or trying to be sorry for something you enjoyed doing, or resolving to avoid actions that bring disagreeable consequences, then what does it mean?

It means, in essence, discovering something about yourself, something positive, not negative. It means realizing that you have potentialities of which you have been so far unaware. It means something within you opening up which hitherto was closed. Suppose I once used to design dust-jackets for novels. It required a certain degree of skill and imagination, and it contented me for quite a long time. Then I began to get bored with it. Occasionally it was more acute than boredom. It was a very painful, though rather inarticulate, sense of frustration. It then occurred to me that I was perhaps wasting my time designing dust-jackets. Maybe I had it in me to be a real painter, perhaps a

81

great painter. If so, then I should have to devote myself
to it completely. I couldn't go on designing dust-jackets
and at the same time give myself away to the visions
of beauty which seemed ready to dance before my eyes.
The moment came when I knew I had to decide one
way or the other. Yet, in another sense, it wasn't really
a decision at all. My power to see in ordinary objects
more than most men see, and to put it on to canvas,
this inner power of mine gave me no rest until I had
surrendered to it. I became a painter, and found a
richer, more satisfying life. More painful than the old
one, certainly liable to agonies unknown before, but
fulfilling and infinitely worthwhile.

That is what repentance means: discovering that you
have more to you than you dreamt or knew, becoming
bored with being only a quarter of what you are and
therefore taking the risk of surrendering to the whole,
and thus finding more abundant life. I'm afraid the
example I gave was a bit highfalutin – it could only
happen to one man in a million. Let's consider something more common: falling in love and marrying. To
begin with I'm contented to live by myself and for myself. What makes me grow tired of this apparently
satisfactory state of affairs? Well, of course, it's Betty
with whom I've fallen in love. But what then has Betty
done as far as I'm concerned? She has evoked my
hitherto dormant capacity to give myself away to
another person. She has made me realize that it is only
by such surrender that I can find my full self and
since it happens that I have done the same for her,
we marry. I have to work harder now than I used to,
in order to support my family. I've sold my car and
buy my suits off the peg. But what are cars and
expensive suits compared with the love which has

enabled me to grow into my proper stature instead of being the dwarf I was in my bachelor days?

What I'm trying to emphasize is that repentance is an inevitable part of all human life, whether people think of themselves as religious or not. Its root is the discovery by us that we are keeping a large part of ourselves locked away, and hence that we are living much more superficially than we need. This discovery is made possible by a vision vouchsafed to us of some good: the hidden beauty of the world in the case of the painter, the lovely person Betty is, in the case of the man who marries. This good, whatever it is, demands surrender to itself. And the consequence of such surrender is a changed life, changed because richer and deeper and more satisfying. And this, because we are using more of what we are and keeping less untapped. And here perhaps we should pause to consider the criticism which Jesus passed on the good religious people of His day. 'The publicans and the harlots,' He told them, 'go into the kingdom of God before you,' and 'there is joy in heaven over one sinner that repenteth more than over ninety and nine righteous persons who need no repentance.' The religious keep their code of morals, and it insulates them from most of what they are. In such a state, they can have no vision, no discontent, no surrender. They keep their talent firmly buried in the earth. They remain a quarter of what they could be. The sinner, on the other hand, tries to live as fully as he can, and discovers by his frustration and despair, how intolerably confining and cramping is the small part of himself which he identifies with the whole of him. This leads him to repentance. He keeps his eyes open for a vision of something better. When it is given to him he surrenders to it, and thereby more of what he is becomes available to him. As always, the result is joy.

But at this point the really vital question obviously is, what are the limits of our potentialities? What have we in us to become? What sort of person shall I be when the whole of me is brought into play? Christians see the answer to this question in Jesus Christ. When, in the gospels, they read of His life and teaching, they recognize themselves. Not themselves as they are, but themselves as they could be.

Take, for example, the most well-known of all the parables, the Good Samaritan. Why is it such a favourite? Because we recognize ourselves in the two chief characters of the story. When I think of what life has done to me in this way and that, especially that I can't be everything I have it in me to be, then I know I am the wounded man left half-dead and needing rescue. But I also know that I am potentially the rescuer as well. The Good Samaritan is a vision of myself. He is me with my deepest capacities no longer hedged in and constricted, but brought into play. He is me fulfilling myself by active compassion for another.

When I can be a person like the Good Samaritan and do what he did, then, I feel, I shall be fully me and abundantly alive. Now throughout His life, Jesus was Himself the Good Samaritan. That is the power which He exercises over us. Jesus is the vision of me as I have it in me to become. And this vision unlocks areas of my being which have so far been inaccessible to me, and even unknown to me. I begin to discover what sort of a person I am, the sort of person who can find his fullness only in self-giving. This discovery is repentance. It brings a change of character, a new and more deeply satisfying life.

84

Christians claim that Jesus was God. As a matter of metaphysics this is impossible to understand. The Christological formulae of the early church councils are obscure. But behind the statement of the doctrine lies something we can all apprehend as absolutely real. Jesus is the vision of man fully himself. And man fully himself shares the life of the Creator, has the same character, engages in the same sort of moral activity. This is quite explicit in Jesus's teaching. 'Be ye therefore merciful, as your Father also is merciful,' 'Love your enemies, bless them that curse you, do good to them that hate you . . . that ye may be the children of your Father which is in heaven : for he maketh his sun to rise on the evil and on the good, and sendeth rain on the just and on the unjust. . . . Be ye therefore perfect, even as your Father which is in heaven is perfect.' What is a father, but he whose nature I share? The ultimate root of repentance is the discovery that we are sons of God, that we have it in us to be what God is like, to be alive as God is alive – by giving, by generosity, by love. It isn't, of course, something which happens to us all of a sudden. I shan't repent for good and all this morning. The vision of myself which is the vision of Jesus (which is the vision of God) will come and go. And when the vision is absent, I shall try to implement what I am by methods which don't work, chiefly by grabbing of one sort or another, instead of by giving. And this will lead me time and time again to frustration and despair. Why, I shall ask bitterly, why has life got to be like this? But it is precisely when I am in this state, wounded and half dead, that the Good Samaritan will once again reveal Himself to me, and thus show me my true identity, as though to say 'You're trying to be like this. But you can't be, because you're really like me.' So I shall repent once more, and again be what I am. This will go on for the whole of our life. For we can't expect to take in something absolutely stupendous all at once. And the good news, the gospel, that we have it in us to be like God, more, to share God's life and partake of His nature, is, in the literal sense of the word, infinitely stupendous. We can assimilate it only slowly and by degrees. That is why repentance is an ever-recurring necessity for us. The discovery of ourselves cannot but continue, because our potentialities are limitless. 'Beloved, now are we the sons of God, and it doth not yet appear what we shall be.'

Conceived and born in sin

We are often told that illusions are merciful, and that to rob people of their illusions is cruel. I don't believe this. I believe that it is the illusions which are cruel and the truth which is merciful. I think, for instance, that nothing is so cruel as the illusion that man is not a fallen creature; and that few things are more merciful than the truth that he is fallen. When you go to a christening, it may shock you to discover that the first words the priest says are, 'Dearly Beloved, forasmuch as all men are conceived and born in sin.' And yet that belief, properly understood, I would claim, is indispensable to all human happiness and maturity.

Of course, words can be terribly misleading. And few words are so utterly misleading as the words 'fallen' and 'sin' in this context. I want, therefore, to make sure that these words are not misunderstood.

We will start with the word 'fallen'.

If I begin by being a Professor at a University and end by teaching at a Preparatory School, you could speak of my decline and fall. Man has not fallen in this sense. He didn't begin great and good, and later become miserable and wicked. If people once believed that, it was because they took the story of the Garden of Eden as literal history. We know now that there never was a Garden of Eden, and that in fact man has evolved from lower forms of life. So the fall is not a fall from a past condition. It is more like a falling short of a future condition. Let me give an example. I have it in me, shall we say, to be a great writer. I feel somehow that I possess this outstanding ability. But, as yet, I haven't been able to actualize it. I haven't been able to give to my writing all I've got. I feel that I could write better than I do, but as yet I can't. This isn't my fault. It's just how things are at the moment. One day, I hope, I *shall* be able to give full expression to my literary potentialities. Until that day comes, I shall continue to fall short of what I fully am.

Now it is in this sense that man is fallen. Man has innate a genius (they call it the image of God), a genius for absolute generosity which is the essence of goodness. But, as yet, man cannot fully actualize this genius. He cannot give himself as he knows he has it in him to give himself. This is not his fault. He was born that way. But, none the less, it makes him fall short of his full stature. He is fallen from what in God's Providence he one day will be.

And now, what about the phrase, 'conceived and born in sin'? First of all, it has nothing to do with the notion that sex is nasty. On the contrary, the church regards sex as God's gracious gift. Nor does 'conceived and born in sin' mean that we came into this world blameworthy, or that our parents were somehow blameworthy for having us. The word 'sin' here has nothing to do with blame at all. It simply means that from the moment of our conception and birth we enter into a state of affairs which is mixed up, a state of affairs to a large extent out of joint. 'Conceived and born in sin' means that, far from being born free, all men everywhere are born in chains. Why this is so, we don't know. We guess at it by myths involving figures like Satan, or the Serpent, or fallen angels. The reason why is hidden from us. But the fact itself stares us in the face everywhere.

You will see how merciful is this truth of the Fall and Original Sin. The best of us are mediocre, to say the least of it. If we imagine we were born unfallen and free, we worry and fret and get angry with ourselves for not being better and greater men than we are. And that is the road to ineffectiveness and breakdown. If, on the other hand, I know that I was born fallen and in sin, I don't hate myself for being as mediocre as I am, since I realize that it is not my fault. And this releases my energies and enables me to grow into maturity and happiness.

I said just now that all men everywhere are born in chains, and that this is what the Fall means.

What are these chains? The chains are something inside me which prevents me from being fully myself. What is this something?

It is a small fraction of what I am which lords it over the rest of me. It is as though one-tenth of my being was a dictator, keeping the other nine-tenths under lock and key.

Let me tell you two stories to illustrate what I mean. They are, of course, imaginary. I was born of drunken parents in the worst sort of industrial slum. From my earliest days I had to live by my wits. I always felt that it was only by being shrewd and calculating that I could hope to survive at all. Thus, as a measure of indispensable security, so it seemed to me, I was forced to stifle all sorts of natural instincts like trust and love and generosity. If I began allowing these free play, I felt I shouldn't survive for an hour. At all costs, I had to keep them under. So here I am now, a spiv, nothing but shrewd and calculating, with an eye to the main chance. So I'm only a tenth of the person I have it in me to be. The me who lives by his wits keeps the rest of me a prisoner. I am in chains.

But now let's go up the social scale. My father is a Member of Parliament, a Junior Minister actually. I always had a good home and I was sent to the best school, and now I'm a member of the best college in the best University. Naturally, I admire my father's success. He has always been keen on success. From my earliest days, success of one sort or another was the certain ticket to his approval. How delighted he was even when I won the silver cup for the high jump at my Private School. I loved having his approval. When it looked as though I'd lost it, life seemed absolutely intolerable. I felt I had to have it, so the self-assertive success-grabbing me took charge of the rest. See me now at parties, cultivating the right friends and making the right remarks. Meet my fiancée, the right gal from the right background. Look at me in church now, asking God to help me go on being a success. I am not a whole man, because my innate capacity for love and leisure and laughter and the joy of living are all kept in chains by the little bit of me concerned with success and grabbing.

So much for our two stories. All of us, in one way or another, stifle what we have it in us to be. We do it without knowing it ('Father, forgive them; for they know not what they do'). And we do it, not because we're wicked, but because we're frightened, frightened of letting ourselves go, frightened of being us, frightened because we don't really believe we're made in the image of God. So frightened, that when a full and perfect man lived on this earth, he had to be killed as a measure

90

of security. And Jesus Christ continues to be crucified inside each of us. And almost certainly we're asking God to help us keep him dead in the interest of a distorted tin-pot picture of Him, which is really a disguise for that part of us which is the dictator. And that is what evil is :

> . . . not, as we thought,
> Deeds that must be punished, but our lack of faith,
> Our dishonest mood of denial,
> The concupiscence of the oppressor.

But we have this hope : Christ's love, which is stronger than our fear, and in the end will prevail. That is the message of the resurrection. And when His love has cast out our fear, then we shall be redeemed, because we shall be fully ourselves.

Christ as the light of the world

Five weeks ago, on Christmas Day, we celebrated the birth of our Lord Jesus Christ. Today we celebrate His being presented to God by His mother in the Temple. An old name for the day is Candlemas. People walked round the church in procession, each carrying a lighted candle. This was an attempt to express in visual form our recognition of Christ as the Light of the World. For it was when as an infant He was being presented to God by His mother in the Temple, that the aged Simeon declared that this child would be a light to lighten the Gentiles, and the glory of God's people, Israel.

So the centre of our worship and thought this morning is Christ as the light of men.

The idea is doubtless familiar. What does it mean in practice?

Christians believe that Jesus Christ is truly God and truly man. We should expect Him therefore to enlighten us about God and about ourselves. And this is what He did, not merely by His teaching (though that is important), but by what He suffered and achieved in His life, death and resurrection.

He was born into a world and into a life similar in

all basic essentials to our own. He was therefore confronted by the perennial perplexities and difficulties of our human lot. We often speak of them as the dark side of life. Of this darkness one of the most persistent forms is the feeling that things are against us.

Let us consider it for a moment.

Perhaps it is our circumstances which are felt to be narrow and frustrating. We never had the opportunities which seem to have come the way of other people. Or perhaps some malignant Fate has struck at us or those we love, bringing disease or death, or some other disaster. Or perhaps nothing much has gone wrong externally, but we feel strongly within ourselves that life is hostile and threatening. We see it in the behaviour of other people towards us which appears indifferent or harsh. Or we see it in the state of the world where nations and groups and classes are fighting desperately for their own interests without thought for others. Or, worst of all, we see it in the contradictions of our own nature which never allow us to be the sort of people we want to be. And although we can't help this, there is none the less a hanging judge within us always determined to condemn us and, if possible, to stifle, or at least to hide, much of what we are.

It is in darkness of this kind that Christ brings us light. He assures us that whatever else may be against us, even if we are against ourselves, God, the most real of all realities, is on our side, not condemning us but taking our part and seeing us through. 'Are not two sparrows sold for a farthing? and one of them shall not fall on the ground without your Father. But the very hairs of your head are all numbered. Fear ye not therefore, ye are of more value than many sparrows.'

In human life, your loving concern for somebody

can't go further than dying for them. In the death of Christ upon the cross we see God's loving concern for us shown forth in this ultimate way. Christ did not die an easy death. He died in great physical pain, and in mental and spiritual agony. The unknowable depths of His sufferings show us the measure of God's love for us. Nothing was held back from us. All was given. And if God is thus for us, who can be against us? He that spared not His own Son, but delivered Him up for us, how shall He not with Him freely give us all things?

But the light of Christ dispels not only the darkness of our hostile world, but also the treacherous shadows of our illusions. For we often misunderstand the ultimate security of God's love for us as something which promises us immediate security against earthly risks. And this is illusion.

What in fact we often want is an abracadabra escape from life, its dangers, sufferings, limitations and question-marks. In the attempt to fulfil this wish, we manufacture an illusory God – a Friend above, with magic powers at his disposal which he will exercise on our behalf; a sort of Aladdin and his wonderful lamp. So long as we keep in with him by trying to be good and moderately religious, then he will protect us from danger, resolve our perplexities, and give us happiness and sufficient prosperity. True, some people will be killed in railway accidents, others will die in slow agony of cancer, others will be driven half mad by the dilemmas which confront them, thousands more will die of starvation in distant continents, but we and those we love, we shall be protected by our all-powerful magician. But then circumstances arise in which our magician fails to act. We rub Aladdin's lamp and no genie appears. We feel let down and angry. What's the use of a God who can't even look after the interests of his own? We'll pay him out by ceasing to believe in him.

What in fact we cease to believe in is our own invention, our wish-fulfilment of a god. And our consequent anger, doubt and despair can be the raw material from which is fashioned genuine faith in the real God, the Father of our Lord Jesus Christ.

It is clear from the gospels that Jesus felt the attraction of the magician-god, felt it as a temptation inevitable for man. Since He was hungry, wouldn't God help Him to turn stones into bread? And if He threw Himself off from the pinnacle of the Temple, wouldn't angels bear Him up? But such thoughts were dismissed as soon as they occurred. To act upon them would be to treat God as less than God, as a serviceable magician. And this would be blasphemy.

Jesus never expected any specially-favoured treatment from life. He recognized and accepted the power exercised over men, and so over Himself, by chance and circumstance. He saw and underlined the enormous part played by necessity or fate in the shaping of human fortune. The Son of man, He said repeatedly, must suffer. His life and message being what it was, the Jews being then what they were, Caiaphas being what he was, Pilate being what he was, the conjunction of circumstances being what it was, Christ saw that His execution was inevitable. And behind all the actors in the drama of His death there lay years of personal history and centuries of national history making them into the sort of people they were. The Son of Man must suffer.

Or again, consider the choice by Jesus of twelve disciples. As man, Jesus was not equipped with magical powers of infallible insight. In choosing the twelve, He submitted Himself to the inevitable risk which all such choices must involve: the risk of making a mistake. And in so doing He brought a terrible disaster upon the head of Judas Iscariot. We must not suppose that His knowledge of it did not form part of His agony in the Garden of Gethsemane. Such risks, with their consequences and afterthoughts, are an inescapable feature of our human condition.

Or again, there is a sense in which all martyrs are responsible for the guilt of their murderers, for it was the martyr's message which provoked the murderer's aggression.

Was it right, was it according to true charity, to provoke the uncompromising hostility of a Caiaphas, or to put a weak-willed Roman Governor into a predicament where he was all but bound to fail in his duty?

Jesus did not seek to escape from such dilemmas as these. He accepted them as humanly necessary. There was no magician on high to release Him from such inevitable tangles. And as He was dying upon the cross, He felt so much the grip of their deadly constraint, that He cried, 'My God, my God, why hast thou forsaken me?'

How do we reconcile God's loving concern for us, shown forth supremely by Christ upon the cross, with the fact that we all must submit to the cruelty of life's contradictions, and that this was true of even Jesus Himself? How can the darkness of our human predicament, which Jesus shared, be the vehicle of God's own marvellous light?

Let us begin with something familiar and use it as a parable.

The artist, be he poet or painter or sculptor, has no

option but to submit to the limitations of his medium.
The necessities of rhythm or rhyme constrain the poet,
the flat surface of the canvas and the properties of
pigment constrain the painter, the hardness of the stone
constrains the sculptor. These things are examples of
brutal necessity from which there is no escape. The
artist, as he must, accepts the brutal necessity. Not
however with stoic resignation. For he uses the
necessity as the very means whereby he achieves his
artistic triumph – the poem, the picture, the sculpture.
And triumph is the word. In submitting to necessity
the artist has conquered it and made it the vehicle of
his creative freedom.

That is what Christ did with human life and death.
He accepted all the brutal necessity in its thousand
different forms. And in accepting it He conquered it,
made it His servant, so that it did what He wanted it
to do: convey the majesty of God's love for men. The
instrument of Christ's total submission to human
bondage – His death upon the cross – is the supreme
achievement which draws men to Him, saying, 'My
Lord and my God.' This is the truth of His resurrection
from the dead. Christ triumphed by making of darkness
the very fuel from which is kindled the light of life.

God loves us supremely and cares for each of us intimately. 'Fear ye not therefore, ye are of more value
than many sparrows.' But this does not mean that He
will wave a magic wand to protect us from misfortune
or to deliver us from human bondage. Life will take
its toll of us, and ever and anon there will be darkness
upon the face of the deep. But if we will, Christ can
open our eyes – we who were born blind – can open
our eyes to perceive the darkness as light, to see necessity
as the means whereby we can obtain our freedom, so

that we shall say, 'We should never have known what love really is, we should never have known what living really is, but for the limitations and contradictions of our human lot, the perplexities and the pain.' That is what Christ does for us, although He does it in unlikely and unimagined ways. He has already begun to do it – for 'God, who commanded the light to shine out of darkness, hath shined in our hearts, to give the light of the knowledge of the glory of God in the face of Jesus Christ.'

Deeper compassion
for humanity

There is one form of compassion which is very important, but which need not detain us long, as it is a matter simply of common-sense and our will. I am thinking of all the humane causes to which we are asked to contribute: the hungry, the blind, the mentally handicapped, and so forth. We cannot give to every cause which appeals for help. But, after thought and prayer, we should decide how much of our income we ought to give away, and then work out our own scheme for doing so. We should be reasonably certain that the causes to which we thus contribute are genuine and reputable. This, as I said, is an important duty. But the manner of doing it is obvious and does not need enlarging upon.

The compassion about which I intend to speak now is not that which is concerned with contributing to causes, but that concerned with the people we meet. It is a deep attitude of heart and mind which involves the whole of what we are. It means that when this or that person happens to cross our path we should be sensitive to understand the nature of their need and identify ourselves with them in this predicament, getting inside their skin, and thus, in the words of St Paul, to rejoice with them that do rejoice and weep with them that weep. This identification of myself with another person, in so far as it is real, is a very costly business – in terms of time and energy, obviously. But also in a much more important and difficult way. Let us put it thus. In spite of our Lord's warning that it is easier for a camel to go through the eye of a needle than for a rich man to enter the kingdom of God, we all of us spend a great deal of our time accumulating riches like crazy. I don't mean money or material possessions. The riches we try to accumulate are those of character and personality. We build up an image of ourselves and one of our main concerns is to keep the fabric in good repair, so that we can confidently say to our own private ear, 'I am this sort of person. I am not that sort of person.' Yet the structure we thus fabricate is, in spite of our apparent confidence, always in a precarious state. Underneath the confidence is the fear of it tumbling down like a house of cards. And this fear inhibits us from feeling any real identity with the man who needs our compassion. For to admit that we are in important respects identical with him seems like removing the bottom card from the card-house or giving it a puff from a pair of bellows. So we treat the other person as a problem or a case or an opportunity to do good instead of as a person of like passions to ourselves, thus keeping him at a safe distance from the image of myself it seems so desperately important to preserve.

Suppose, for instance, that we come across a kleptomaniac. We may be enlightened enough to realize that simply to condemn him as a criminal does no good to anybody. Instead we may think of him and behave towards him as somebody who has a disease called kleptomania, like a man who has the measles. But this apparently enlightened, clinical approach is in fact an attempt to prevent ourselves from perceiving how much we have in common with him. For his stealing is an attempt to compensate himself for an intolerable sense of having no value, and this sense of having no value follows from his never having been properly loved. Now none of us has been fully loved. It is true of all of us that in this way or that way, to this degree or that degree, the love we needed to feel our own value has been withheld. And so the spectre of valuelessness haunts us all, waiting to spring. And quite a lot of the things I do are attempts to avert my gaze from this ghost who would take from me all reasons for living. True, my own way of compensating myself for the threatening sense of valuelessness is not that of the kleptomaniac. I do not go around shop-lifting. But I see to it none the less that I accumulate quite a lot of riches : I'm a good sort, I have friends who like me, I get a First in the Tripos, I have a strong will, I went to an expensive school, I have working-class parents, I have a girl-friend who is acknowledged to be exceptionally pretty, I have had a lot of sex, I am a pillar of the college chapel, I am a man of prayer and people realize I live close to God. Now all this sort of riches builds up an impenetrable barrier between myself and the kleptomaniac. For what he needs is somebody who will relinquish these mirages and brave the appalling desert of valuelessness, where he and I both in fact really are. It is in the acknowledgement of this common bond, in the realization that he and I are in the same hell, that true compassion is born and grows. It is not that I am healthy and he is diseased. We both suffer from the same wounds, and that is how we can meet and communicate with each other.

101

'There, but for the grace of God, go I' sounds pious, but it speaks not of compassion but of superiority. Compassion says, 'There, by the grace of God, I have been and I am.' It is in this sense surely that we should understand St Paul's words about Jesus: that God 'made him to be sin for us, who knew no sin,' or St Matthew's words, echoing Isaiah: 'Himself took our infirmities, and bare our sicknesses.' 'Christ,' said Calvin, 'endured in his soul the dreadful torments of a condemned and lost man.' The reason why we fail in compassion is because we are too frightened thus to follow Jesus to the cross, going forth unto Him bearing His reproach, filling up our share in His afflictions.

Now I know this may sound masochistic, and there is no doubt that what I have said could be twisted to serve the interests of that kind of emotional disorder. But the Christian experience is totally different. Let me put it this way. The Christian gospel speaks a lot about Good Friday and of its inevitability. But for Christian faith Good Friday is seen in the context of Easter. If Christ died, He died in order that He might be raised from the dead. And in page after page of the New Testament we are told that in so far as we share in Christ's sufferings we are made partakers here and now of His resurrection. This is the great and glorious paradox of Christian experience: that it is by dying that we live, that it is by sharing with Jesus the horror of His agony that we live with Him reigning indestructibly in peace. Once we are willing to see and feel the desert in which we live, the desert becomes fertile, bringing forth every tree whose fruit shall be for meat, and the leaf thereof for healing. Once we know that we are poor, the kingdom of Heaven is ours. So when our lot is cast with somebody who is finding his cross, his desert, his poverty overwhelming, we are on holy ground. For it is precisely here that God is present to save, to save us as well as them. So our identification with the other person brings to our lives and to their's the power, the joy, the victory which is already ours and all mankind's in Christ Jesus Our Lord.

That, I believe, is the message which our age is waiting to hear – a realistic recognition of suffering and evil in the universe, not trying apologetically to pretend that things are better than they are, together with the first-hand affirmation of this suffering and evil as the place where the Son of Man is glorified and with Him we and all mankind.

In a few moments we shall be singing the *Sanctus,* the song of the cherubim and the eternal music of the spheres. And that is what Gethsemane and Calvary mean, because that is what God has made of them. That 'stinking fosse where the injured Lead the ugly life of the rejected' – that ditch is the Church of the Holy Sepulchre. That is why we can be nearer to God in Tangier than in Canterbury. And when we Christian people fail in compassion it may be because we are too concerned to prove to ourselves that Canterbury is where we live. 'Could ye not watch with me one hour? And they all forsook him and fled.' But God grant us the courage to stay with Jesus so that we may know the power of His resurrection and the fellowship of His sufferings, and thereby transmit to those we meet some of the riches of His compassion.

God is charity

A fundamental Christian assertion is that God is charity. There is also a well-known phrase, 'As cold as charity'. Now of course, in that phrase charity does not mean love. It means the mechanical administration of alms-giving. You put in the plate a ten shillings you can well afford, and you don't have to be mixed up with the irritating human beings your money is going to help. Needless to say, nobody imagines that God's charity is like that. But I think we can, none the less, still use the phrase, 'as cold as charity' – 'as cold as the divine charity', 'as cold as God's love'. I don't mean that God's love is in fact cold. It's much too hot for most of us most of the time. But it is often made to appear cold by those who are afraid of its heat and are on the look-out for respectable reasons for cooling it down. Thus, for instance, we are often told that God's love is totally different from natural love. The warmth, the thrill, the vital peace, of satisfactory natural love have nothing in common with true love for God, let alone God's attitude to us. Our love for God is a matter of will-power, not of anything we know as love at all. And as for God's attitude to us, it's cold and austere. At Cana of Galilee Jesus turned water into wine. Most of us Christians spend a great deal of our time trying to turn wine into water. With regard to much human feeling, we attempt to damp it down, and if we succeed we call this negative result goodness. And we think that God is pleased, for most of us, somewhere in our heart, keep an idol of a cold-austere schoolmaster of a God. That is the chief reason, perhaps the only reason, why we sin. We deeply resent having this inhuman monster as Lord over us. To thumb-nose and kick Him is our secret pleasure, secret, very often, even from ourselves. Sometimes it breaks out into the open – especially in undergraduate magazines or television programmes, where there appears something which is openly blasphemous. But what it blasphemes against is the idol, not the true God, so the blasphemy is really a worship of the true by a making fun of the false. For when you think of a working-class woman having a baby in what are virtually slum conditions, or if you think of a man without a home, who in the end was unjustly condemned to the gallows by church people, there is nothing to sneer at or to thumb-nose. And that is the true God we worship, the God of Bethlehem, and of Calvary.

God's coming to us in the humanity of Jesus shows that His charity is the most human thing conceivable, warm, sweet, tender, as the hymn has it. That is because being human is not a shabby thing to be ashamed of. For us human beings being human is God's gift of Himself, the way in which His charity operates. Our being human is God increasing joy. Go into a Lyons teashop with a friend. As you eat your bun together and drink your coffee, surrounded by a crowd of people, Lyons is Emmaus. Christ is present in this breaking of the bread. His love envelops you. He can make Himself known to you without your being explicitly aware of it. All you may feel is the warmth of companionship. But, when you come to think about it later, your happiness showed that Christ was there. Do you know John

105

Betjeman's poem, *In a Bath Teashop?*

'Let us not speak, for the love we bear one another—
    Let us hold hands and look.'
She, such a very ordinary little woman;
    He, such a thumping crook;
But both, for a moment, little lower than the angels
    In the teashop's ingle-nook.

That is the divine charity.

Somebody in London said to me the other day that he disliked the Holy Communion because it was too personal. Lucky man. He was an accountant, so he hadn't the theological *savoir-faire* to explain away his phobia by respectable academic arguments about the nature of Godhead. He just admitted he was afraid of being a person. I know what he meant. Personal encounter of any kind can be terrifying. That is why people want to depersonalize God's love and play it cool. Otherwise, it is felt to be too threatening. The conventions of polite society, social etiquette and so forth, are a device to protect people from the onslaught of personal encounter. I can't play this game properly, but I've seen it played with exquisite skill and grace, so that people in a room together never meet each other at all. I think that quite a lot of the religious programmes and rules we adopt are parallel to social etiquette. They help us not to meet the personal, human charity of God. We escape from the real world, where we meet God's charity in what we are and in what other people are, escape into an alternative, less threatening world, called religion and church.

Why do we fear personal encounter? Well, I think it is this: it is true of practically all of us that somewhere, sometime – and almost certainly we've forgotten it –

somewhere, sometime, our intrinsic tenderness has been violated. For us, therefore, encounter spells violation. A poet reads his most sacred secrets to an audience which laughs and jeers. A lover tells of his deepest feelings to be scoffed at and condemned. A child lifts up his face to be kissed and hugged, and is told to go back into the nursery. An infant stretches out its hands to its universe (its mother) to be repelled. Once bitten, twice shy. If personal encounter means such violation of tenderness, then the pain is too great, the cost too high. Let us see it doesn't happen again. Let us depersonalize ourselves so as to avoid the agony of personal encounter.

Now God's Charity won't let you stick there. He has created me to be a person, and He will carry on His work. His aim is to make me capable of the happiness He planned to give me before the foundation of the world. But to do it He must lead me to open my wounds so that He can heal them. And this opening of wounds is always painful. Perhaps we may put it thus : God has created the whole of what I am, so He won't allow me to keep part of myself anaesthetized. He wakes up what I would keep asleep, and the result is inner conflict. This terrible concern of God for the whole of me is what I believe is meant by His wrath. He won't let sleeping dogs lie because He knows that I can't be truly happy unless and until I am fully myself. When I have learnt to receive what I would now refuse, then there will be no more conflict. But it takes time, probably a lifetime. This is what I have called the opening of wounds. God does it for us by means of our ordinary experience of life – by our succeeding, working, failing, falling in love, getting into a stew, feeling angry – the whole kaleidoscope of living. And when this is happening it feels as though God isn't there. His charity seems an illusion. If God cared, how could He let us endure such things and be reduced to such a state? What is hidden from us is God's concern that nothing we are should be lost. Here I want to quote some remarkable words of Proust. 'When,' says Proust, 'in the course of my life, I have had occasion to meet with, in convents, for instance, literally saintly examples of practical charity, they have generally had the brisk, decided, undisturbed, and slightly brutal air of a busy surgeon, the face in which one can discern no commiseration, no tenderness at the sight of suffering humanity and no fear of hurting it, the face devoid of gentleness or sympathy, the sublime face of true goodness.' That is how God's love can feel like when He is opening our wounds to heal them. Like a great surgeon, He has no fear of hurting us because of His absolute competence to make us well. The knife is securely in His hands. In the operating theatre, the surgeon's face only *looks* devoid of gentleness of sympathy, for his whole work, his entire commitment and vocation, flows from his desire to help and to heal. And there can be no deeper sympathy than that, no more effective gentleness. The God we worship has shown forth His sympathy and gentleness, His Charity, by being wounded Himself in order the better to heal us—

> The wounded surgeon plies the steel
> That questions the distempered part;
> Beneath the bleeding hands we feel
> The sharp compassion of the healer's art
> Resolving the enigma of the fever chart.

So we must not be taken in when it feels as if God doesn't care. For in fact He is allowing us to be turned inside out and shaken upside down in order to give us the openness to life, the ability to receive life without fear, which belongs to a full person. We must not worry about it with fretful scheming. We must trust God to do it for us because He is Charity. The world is charged with the grandeur of God. It will flame out. Because the Holy Ghost over the bent world broods with warm breast. Our world, the world which is us – all we are and do and suffer. There is Charity flaming out, creating us. For God's charity is not a sort of wireless wave or spiritual chemical. It comes to us incarnated, inseparably bound up with our whole human experience. It is by means of our living our human lives in this world that God is creating us.

But if charity is thus to create you, you mustn't protect yourself from it behind the shelter of the preconceived idea. What I mean is you mustn't start with the assumption that charity must always involve a certain set of particular actions, or must never involve another set of particular actions. For in this case charity ceases to be itself and becomes the slave of a culture. Sixty years ago many of the upper and middle classes sincerely believed that charity involved never going on strike. Today, the Roman Catholic Church still believes that true charity between husband and wife forbids the practice of contraception. Be careful of the commands and prohibitions which are said to protect charity, for such protection sometimes turns out in fact to be protective custody, because charity threatens the vested interests of the *status quo*. If you want the point further elucidated, read the works of the Catholic novelist, Graham Greene. Few people in our time, have understood so profoundly or set out so illuminatingly what it means to resist Charity or to be created by it.

Another thing to remember is that Charity is God's

giving His isness to you. In consequence you find your-self the sort of person who really loves other people instead of the sort of person who tries to act as though he did. When people say that I acted charitably towards so and so, what they generally mean is that in fact I hate his guts but managed to behave as though I didn't. This use of the word in common parlance is a sign of disbelief in God's ability really to change me, as if to say that He can't alter me fundamentally, but only supply me with a sort of spiritual benzedrine which enables me to perform feats beyond my natural condition. 'Charity tries to suffer long, charity tries to be kind, it tries not to envy, it tries to be not easily provoked. Charity tries to bear all things, tries to be-lieve all things, tries to hope all things, tries to endure all things.' That is how in our mind we re-write St Paul's great chapter. But Charity doesn't try. It is, because God is. That is the miracle to belief in which all Christians everywhere are fundamentally committed – the miracle of our becoming like God by sharing His life.

Now what I have just said is often confused with something very different, namely, that we should always give way to the impulse of the moment. But nobody could live at all in society if they did this. Discipline and self-control are essential. But they are of two kinds and spring from two sources. In the words of Jesus, one kind imposes heavy burdens, grievous to be borne, and lays them upon men's shoulders. The other kind is described in the words, 'My yoke is easy, and my burden is light'. Suppose, for example, that I came from a family of competent scientists, and my father expected me to carry on the family tradition. As it happens, my real interests are in literature, not science. But in loyalty to my family and in obedience to my

110

father's wishes I go slogging away preparing for the Natural Sciences Tripos. I discipline myself to do ten hours work a day. But I don't make any progress and the discipline is making me depressed and on edge. In the end it becomes too much for me to bear and I leave Cambridge. My work has been one long denial of what I really am, for my real interests are literary. But suppose, on the contrary, that I was studying for the English Tripos. My work would still require effort, discipline, and self-control. For to go to the cinema or the pub would often seem more immediately inviting than studying Milton. Yet because of my literary interests and abilities, the discipline I impose upon myself is not a perpetual denial of what I am but a perpetual affirmation of it. So, although I do a great deal of work, I am profoundly happy and grow in stature as a person. Charity's discipline is of this second kind. It is a constant self-affirmation, like a pianist devoted to his art, who will do anything, however laborious, and give up anything, however attractive, in order to perfect his technique, and thereby find his life. Once we are certain that a discipline enables us to be ourselves, to share God's isness, the yoke will be easy and the burden light, whatever it entails.

The Christian gospel is the assertion that God creates us the sort of people to whom Charity is natural, a self-affirmation. Jesus, we are told, for the joy that was set before Him, endured the Cross – charity at its completest and most absolute. And Jesus gives His Spirit to us – or so, at least, we claim to believe.

> The Angel that presided o'er my birth
> Said 'Little creature, form'd of joy and mirth,
> Go, love without the help of anything on earth.'

111

Life abundant
or
life resisting?

In 1927, that is before the character and methods of Soviet Russia were fully appreciated in the West and before the rise of Hitler in Germany, a member of Trinity, then a past Fellow, declared in a published statement, 'I say quite deliberately that the Christian religion as organized in its churches has been and still is the principal enemy of moral progress in the world.'

In more recent times, Lord Russell has been concerned with what he considers still greater evils, but, none the less, as a Christian, I believe that there is a disturbing amount of truth in the indictment he brought some thirty years ago. Naturally I do not believe it is the whole truth nor the most important part of it. Whatever moral progress means, I suppose (to take one example) that the abolition of slavery and active concern for the poor and outcast, such practical insistence upon the absolute value of human persons, is a sign of moral progress, and this owes a very great deal to the Christian religion as organized in its churches.

No purpose, however, is served in trying to draw up

112

from the past a statement of account in order to show that Christianity is not in the moral red. The task is impossible. The precise knowledge required is not available. But what we can do, and if we are sincere we must do, is to examine the Christianity which we now profess.

So let me go straight to the point with the question: does our Christianity make for a better and a happier world, or does it not?

Well, frankly, I believe that quite often it does not, that Christianity in many of its forms is not a good but an evil thing. I am not thinking of Christians failing to live up to the ideals they profess. That is universal among men. Nor am I thinking in terms of the more obvious classifications of Christianity into, shall we say, Roman Catholicism or American Revivalism. The evil is too subtle to be so easily identifiable, and it can be found in all branches of the Christian Church, in every type and sect of Christianity.

Perhaps the root of the trouble is this: the habit of mind which makes us think of God as one item in His universe, as one object among other objects, in the sense in which, for example, a newspaper might declare itself as being for God, King and country, or a theologian might say that although he is interested in many things God is his chief interest, or a devout person might say that he gives so much time to his work, so much to recreation, and so much to God. Thinking in this way, God is conceived as one being among a multitude of other beings, who stands over against us and is this and not that, here and not there. I have called this a habit of mind. But it is not really an intellectual error, a mistake avoided by the more intelligent among us. Fundamentally it is a failure not

113

in intelligence but in love. It is due to an insufficient apprehension of the charity which is God. And it is the very meaning of our self-inflicted exile from our home, and so from our fulfilment and our peace.

Let us first see some of the damaging results which follow.

If God is one item in His universe, then religion is a departmental activity, a recreation or a task among other recreations and tasks. With the best will in the world, this drives a thick wedge between religion and life and perfectly justifies the man who says that he is no more interested in religion than he is in golf. We all know the type of God-enthusiast who rushes round trying to make other people religious. To many, he is as great a bore as the golf-enthusiast. But there is this difference. Unless he is a lunatic, the golf-enthusiast realizes that, in the last resort, his game is not the most important thing in the world. But the God-enthusiast is convinced that everything in heaven and earth must be subordinated to the demands of his game. And the results can be ugly and inhuman.

Or again, if God is one object among others, then He may assume the character of an alternative. I want so and so – success, popularity, sex, or whatever it is. I can't get it. So I will have God instead. This produces a passive attitude towards life which inhibits all growth of personality. It was to a large extent because he thought that belief in a God was inevitably bound up with such passivity that Freud rejected all religion as pathological. And of course when God is considered as the easier because always available alternative to something or somebody else, then Freud is right. Religion does keep us permanently immature.

Or once again, the God who is a being standing over

against us, because he is our own invention, is made in our own image. This means, first of all, that we project our own feelings of insecurity upon the Heavens. There is, shall we say, some discovery, some new form of knowledge, and it contains a threat – a threat, that is, to ourselves as committed to untenable ideas and attitudes. But we shan't think of it like that. The threat, we shall think, is to God Himself – as indeed it is to the God of our own invention. So we shall rush to God's defence. We can see this process encapsulated in the nineteenth-century controversy between religion and science. True, the discoveries of those days are now accepted by the vast majority of Christians. But let no one imagine that we have therefore ceased resisting the Holy Ghost. The God of our invention is still threatened by the new knowledge. This time it is by discoveries about the emotional roots of human character and behaviour, and still we are rushing to the defence of our idol – that is, of ourselves.

This idol, so we often think, is the creator of only a part of us – that part of us which we do not hesitate to display in public, the respectable civilized part of us. He is not, we think, responsible for those instinctive drives which are the strongest things we know. Indeed, he is somehow in competition with them. And, as an omnipotent competitor, he is able to beat us from the start by saying, 'Thou shalt not,' and backing up his prohibitions by the most absolute of all sanctions : not capital punishment but eternal torment. So we have to mortify half our being, to kill it. Mercifully, however, life is stronger than death, and ever and anon asserts itself in glorious witness to the true God who is the creator of the whole of us: 'The awful daring of a moment's surrender, which an age of prudence can never retract, by this and this only, we have existed.'

But our invented God will fight back, and hit as hard as he can. How dare we be ourselves? How dare we function as we are made to function? How dare we give expression to that part of us which our God did not create? How dare we choose that, in preference to him?

So we may feel very frightened. And thereby confuse virtue with being on the side of the big battalions. And meanwhile there will probably be some Christian pundit or other to tell us that we must not misunderstand the affirmation that God is love. True, he wants us to love him. But if he can't get us by love, he'll get us by fear. Which is like saying, 'Love me, or I'll beat you till you do.' And isn't something of this sort rather like what, in our weakness and imperfection, we ourselves sometimes feel about the people we want to love us, but who don't?

All the same, if such insidious evils often creep into our Christianity, and sometimes dominate it, thereby making the world a worse and less happy place, that is not the whole truth nor the most important part of it.

For the habit of mind which thinks of God as somebody over there who must not be neglected nor his wishes disobeyed – this habit of mind does not always prevail within us. The divine charity does not leave itself altogether without witness in our hearts, and when men are possessed by charity then they are capable of producing things that are good and lovely. It is difficult to talk about, since charity surpasses knowledge. It transcends theological definition. Certainly it is not a correct account of things, a piece of information which can be handed on like a mathematical formula or kitchen recipe. We can know it only in so far as we have experience of it. But then we have, all of us, had

116

experience of it, whether we deny that we are Christians or claim that we are. For the true light lighteneth every man that cometh into the world.

Perhaps we may put it thus: we all have experience of two types of feeling. There is the feeling which unites us to our world and makes us rejoice in it – an experience of love, of acceptance, of communion. And there is the other kind of feeling which separates us from our world and makes us hate it – an experience of fear, of exile, of discord. The first of these feelings belongs more truly to us than the second. We are profoundly satisfied by love and communion. We are exasperated by exile and hatred. The first convinces us that things are right with us. The second convinces us that things are wrong with us. It would seem as though we were born with a consent to love and communion and that it is only when something prevents their growth and fruition that they turn into hatred and alienation.

The difference between these two types of feeling is the difference between good and evil, and evil is secondary, existing not in its own right but as thwarted goodness.

The good feeling, the feeling which unites us to the world and makes us rejoice in it, is the divine charity. It is God. And it is God experienced throughout the whole area of human life and activity.

Let us see what this means in practice.

The joy which a man finds in his work and which transforms the tears and sweat of it into happiness and delight – that joy is God. The wonder and curiosity which welcomes what is new and regards it not as threatening but enriching life – that wonder and curiosity is God. The confidence which leads us to abandon the shelter of our disguises and to open up the doors of our personality so that others may enter there, and both we and they be richer for the contact – that confidence is God. The vision which enables us to see the majesty of men, of all men including ourselves, piercing through the ugliness of the obscuring pathology to the beauty of the real person – that power of vision is God. The sense of belonging to the natural world, the exhilarating certainty that all things are ours whether things in heaven or things on the earth – that sense of belonging is God. The superabundance which leads us naturally and inevitably to give, not as a matter of duty nor in a spirit of patronage, but because we cannot forbear – that superabundance is God. The compelling conviction that in spite of all evidence to the contrary, in spite of all the suffering we may have to witness or to undergo, the universe is on our side, and works not for our destruction but for our fulfilment – that compelling conviction is God.

In experiences of this sort, which occur to all of us whether or not we are technically religious, it is as though we were receiving something, as though we were reaching forth to embrace a richness greater than ourselves. Greater implies other. Yet what we receive does not turn us into paupers who cannot work their own passage. On the contrary, it is in such receiving that we are most alive, most ourselves, most capable of great achievement and high endeavour. That is because God is the ground of our being, whose imparting of Himself makes us what we are and establishes our personal identity. And because this is so, the alternative, God or man, is false. This is particularly important in these days when we are apt to think, 'My experience of the worthwhileness of life, of gladness, of adventure, of communion, of love, this is not God. It's just my

118

emotions, or it's just sex – something which can be explained away by biochemistry, or psychology.'

Of course it is our physical make-up. Of course it is our emotions. Of course it is sex. Very much more so, probably, than we understand, or, in our stupid suburban spiritual snobbery, are willing to admit even to ourselves. Of course it is everything we are. But then, everything we are is God imparting Himself to us, and therefore in everything we are we feel after Him and find Him. The whole of us flows from the one fountain of life, and it is by means of the whole of us that we return to the source from which we have sprung.

It is because religion in the true sense is as comprehensive as life itself that we cannot find God or serve Him or love Him with a mere part of ourselves – let us say, by a mere effort of will, by gritting the teeth and clenching the fist. What we most truly are in the depths of our being refuses to surrender to force – force from within no more than force from without. That is what St Augustine meant when he said that Christ's command to love God is not obeyed if it is obeyed as a command. That is what St Paul meant when he said, 'Though I bestow all my goods to feed the poor, and though I give my body to be burned, and have not charity, it profiteth me nothing.'

Nor can we find Him in whom we live and move and have our being simply by the exercise of our intelligence. You will remember in Hans Andersen's story of the Snow Queen, how little Kay with the ice-blocks of reason could never find out how to place them in order to form a word he was most anxious to make, the word 'Eternity'. The fact is that although the claims of the intellect are pretentious, its bag is disappointing. It has to kill the living reality before it can make it its

119

own. Thought is always a post-mortem. That was what St Paul meant when he said, 'Though I . . . understand all mysteries . . . and all knowledge . . . and have not charity, I am nothing.'

Nor can we find God merely by being religious in the narrow technical sense. Eight hundred years before Christ, the prophets of Israel proclaimed this fact when they condemned as useless the religious ritual of their day. But ritual need not be external. It can take the form of devotional clichés, or the manipulating of people so as to produce in them a certain type of psychological experience. Religion, in this sense, is not enough. For 'Though I speak with the tongues of men and of angels . . . though I have the gift of prophecy . . . though I have all faith, so that I could remove mountains, and have not charity, I am nothing.'

Charity is not consequence. It is not reward. Charity is gift, God's gift of Himself to us, the gift which makes us what we are. And we do not receive it in any specialized activity abstracted from the rest of our lives. For God gives Himself to us in everything, including our own nature. In our own capacity to feel, to think, to criticize, to condemn, to love, to resolve, to endure – there is God giving Himself to us, there is that most excellent gift of charity.

Charity is the power to accept, to accept ourselves and other people and the world as the presence of God. Charity is the power not to deny but to affirm experience, not to shrink away from it in frozen or indignant alarm but to go out and meet it, because, in spite of the apparent threats and dangers, it is our creator, come, not to steal, nor to kill, nor to destroy, but that we might have life and have it more abundantly.

120

The Trinity

You will, I hope, forgive a preacher in this place on Trinity Sunday for feeling it would be a neglect of duty, should he fail to preach on the doctrine of the Three Persons and One God. I do not, however, intend to tire you for long with abstract theology. Although I must first indicate in a few words how the Church Universal thinks of the Trinity, my main purpose this evening will be to enquire into the compelling appeal which this doctrine undoubtedly exercised upon Christendom for countless centuries. If it doesn't exercise such appeal today, and it manifestly doesn't, that is only one striking example of the decay and death of religious images. If we could learn what was the appeal of the image of the Trinity, we might be able to re-establish it in the hearts of Christian folk. I believe that all doctrines, including Christian doctrines, are like Merovingian emperors. To understand why men are prepared to live for them and die for them, it is necessary to discover who is the Mayor of the Palace. To speak more plainly, what are men affirming about themselves, inarticulately but passionately, in the doctrines to which they give their whole-hearted allegiance? That is not the only question which could be asked. But for the post-Freudian world it is the inevitable question. When, in our times, Christian thinkers avoid it, they tend to become mere idle singers of an empty day. What are men affirming about themselves? It is a particularly pertinent question to ask about the doctrine of the Trinity. For it was in a treatise on this very subject, written in the early years of the fifth century, that the most influential theologian of the Church conducted so profound a self-analysis that it led him to discover and describe what we now call the unconscious, as Professor J. Burnaby has pointed out in his recent edition of St Augustine's *De Trinitate*.

But first the doctrine in its abstract form. Here there are two main approaches. One of them, the less orthodox, treats the three persons of the Godhead as though they were persons more or less in our sense of the word, three personalities. How then can these three be one? We are wrong, it is argued, in thinking of oneness in terms of mathematical oneness. For here oneness, by definition, excludes multiplicity. But there are other kinds of oneness which, far from excluding multiplicity, demand it. There is, for instance, the oneness of a living organism or the oneness of a work of art. And these, it is said, provide us with a better analogy for the Oneness of God than the abstract symbols of mathematics. On this view, Father, Son and Holy Ghost, are each of them a personality. But they are so perfectly united, so absolutely do they interpenetrate each other, that they form one single divine life. In our own human experience we come nearest to such a unity – though it is but a faint reflection of it – when we are so closely bound up with another person that we share by instinct their deepest thoughts and feelings.

However, this view of the Trinity is open to serious criticism. In the formula, three persons and one God, the Greek word, *hypostasis* translated 'person', doesn't

122

necessarily mean a person in our sense at all, a personality. It merely means a subject on which verbs can be hung. Anything about which statements can be made is a *hypostasis,* a person in the language of the formula – your shoes, for instance, or my spectacles. Thus, to say that God is three persons does not mean that each of these is a person in our sense, a personality. If, as we say, God is personal, He is One Person, not three. But in the One person there are three modes of being, three subjects about which statements can be made. Each subject is personal, not because each is, in our sense, a person but because each is God and God is personal. The best analogy has been provided by St Augustine. I can speak of my memory, my understanding, and my will. Each of these is a subject about which statements can be made. And each of these is personal, not because I am three people but because the single person I am energizes in these three ways. My memory is me, my understanding is me, and my will is me. Yet each of these must be differentiated from the other. And this may point to the possibility of God being three as well as one.

So much for the formal statement of the doctrine. Thus formulated, it exercises a certain kind of appeal for a certain kind of mind. But it most certainly isn't a matter of living faith or ultimate concern. It seems little more than a theological brain-twister, not something to live and die for.

What then gave it the immense attraction it once possessed? I'm not attempting to describe how the belief arose. Nor am I trying to explain it away. I am asking simply why something which now seems lifeless was felt for a long period to be the very secret of life. Let us revert to our Merovingian Emperor. We have seen him in the formal statement of the doctrine. His regalia to us looks slightly ridiculous, and in his stiff formality he is powerless to enlighten us. Can we leave him for the back rooms in order to find the Mayor of the Palace?

I suspect that the doctrine of the Trinity was felt to meet two threats to which every human being is subject, two threats, each of which, if fully implemented, would destroy us. I notice that a great deal of what we do is concerned with meeting and overcoming these threats, and that this is a matter both of instinct and of conscious contrivance. I suspect that the doctrine of the Trinity was felt as something like a promise or guarantee that these two threats would be finally overcome. So that the cry from the heart, 'I am not made for destruction,' was felt to be symbolized or schematized in the doctrine of the Three in One. The two threats are the threat of isolation, on the one hand, and the threat of absorption, on the other. Each is a potential murderer. Let us consider them in turn.

It is obvious that, in infancy, isolation from our world, even though our world consist only of a mother, would biologically be disastrous. We are entirely dependent upon it for food and protection, for everything. As we grow up, our dependence does not so much diminish as change its area. Even in the Garden of Eden, with all the material necessities of life provided, the Lord God said, 'It is not good that the man should be alone.' Relationship with other people offers us, of course, positive good. But on its negative side it is our response to the threat of being isolated. In sex this is instinctive. That is why a person seriously crossed in love feels isolated from everybody and everything. In the words of the popular song, recently revived by Eartha Kitt, 'The blues is nothing but a one way ticket from your love to nowhere'. Or again, the moral discipline we impose upon ourselves finds much of its dynamic in the threat of our being abandoned and left to rot on our own. If we do so and so, society will kick us out, or God will give us up and cease to look after us, or (to say the same thing in different language) we shall be isolated from that part of us whose approval we solicit. Or again, what is the basic motive of ambition, of wanting to be top people? No doubt it is mixed; but one of the chief elements is the often unrecognized fantasy that we shall be liked or loved because we are successful, and to that degree, our ambition is a precaution against being isolated. And then there is the fear of death, common to all men. 'Men fear death,' said Bacon, 'as children fear to go in the dark.' And what is fear of the dark but fear of isolation, the dread of aloneness, instinctively externalized into a hundred unimaginable monsters? There is no need to multiply examples. The point is obvious enough. From the moment of our birth, we fear the threat of isolation, and a great deal of what we do is motivated by the need to take precautions against it.

At the same time, however, there is the opposite danger, the danger of our being absorbed, absorbed into what promises to extinguish our individuality. You may remember the well-known lines,

> Like many of the upper class
> He liked the sound of broken glass.

The urge to beat up the place is in part stimulated by the threat of being absorbed into a set-up so that I become no longer myself but just an expression of the set-up.

Or again, the maddening demand for continuous

attention which, as every uncle knows, is universal among small children, is really a manifesto: 'I'm not just part of the house and garden, I'm me. I'm horribly me.' And you can very often observe much the same thing at a dinner table when people try to monopolize the conversation in order to prove that they haven't become assimilated to the furniture. And how many wives, husbands, children, friends, employees, and subordinates have not sometimes in a fit of anger said (even if the conversation is only imaginary), 'Don't think that I'm the sort of person who will sit down under this sort of thing.' Admittedly, these are all trifles. But then a man can be hanged for a finger-print. They indicate something much more important than themselves. They help to show, for instance, how a sincerely religious person can be, in the usual sense, bitterly anti-religious. If I feel that religion is a threat to my individuality, then, if I am a person of any integrity, my religion must consist of opposing religion tooth and nail. This, I suppose, is what Clemenceau meant where he said, 'There's only one thing worse than a bad priest, and that's a good one.' Marriages often break down because one partner feels that the other is trying to absorb him or her. Think how much has been said and written about the jealous wife or husband. Colleagues quarrel with each other because their point of view is not recognized. And death is feared, not only as the isolator but as the final absorber. As the traditional language has it, we return to the dust of which we are made.

Isolation, absorption. Being human means being poised between these two anxieties, these two threats, each of which is felt as capable of exterminating us. And that is the ultimate threat: extermination, the triumph of non-being over being.

126

In the doctrine of the Trinity we have set before us an image in which this threat of non-being, in its two chief forms, is met and overcome. The threat of being isolated is overcome because the One God is described as being eternally in relation. That, I suggest, is the significance of our belief in God as Father, Son, and Holy Ghost. Our heart protests that we were not made for the death which comes from being isolated. And so, what better picture is there of the fount of our being, of the source from which we spring, of our ultimate refuge, of the rock that is higher than me? What better picture than the God who, although He is One, is also eternally Three? For where there is relatedness there can be no aloneness. At the same time the doctrine of the Trinity provides us with an image in which the opposite threat of absorption is met and vanquished. The persons of the Godhead are for ever distinct and unconfused. The Son and the Spirit cannot be absorbed into the Father. From all eternity to all eternity they are what they are.

The meeting and overcoming of this threat of destruction, of non-being, in its two forms is something after which men hunger and thirst, as their behaviour clearly shows. The doctrine of the Trinity asserts that in Being Itself, in God, this threat of non-being is for ever encountered and for ever conquered. This, surely, is the compelling attraction of Trinitarian doctrine, what makes it a matter of living faith and ultimate concern, 'O death, where is thy sting? O grave, where is thy victory?'

What I am suggesting is that if men feel after God and find Him, they do so at a level of their being far deeper than that of their discursive reason. Their thinking is no more than a formal schematization of what they feel, a schematization which often looks slightly absurd. For the heart is wiser than the head, and knows more. I didn't begin with a text, so I will end with one. 'We know that, when God shall appear, we shall be like Him, for we shall see Him as He is.'

So it is with our belief in God the Trinity.

Revelation

The Hulsean Preacher is bidden by the Ordinances of the University to deliver a sermon on the Truth and Excellence of Revealed Religion. I want this morning to consider two aspects of God's revelation of Himself in Christ, one of which is considered by all Christians everywhere to be fundamental to their faith, the other by almost all. The first is the belief that the one and only God is the Creator and that it was this same God who was made man in Jesus Christ. The second is the belief that when God thus took manhood to Himself, the human nature He assumed was not stifled or destroyed by His Divinity, but came to its full and perfect expression.

It might well seem a waste of time to commend beliefs we all hold, to urge acceptance of truths which no Christian within striking distance wishes to deny. Preaching to the converted may give pleasure to the preacher, but it will certainly bore his audience, unless their conversion is not so complete as they imagine. But this, I believe, is in fact often precisely the case with regard to the two doctrines we are discussing. St Paul said of himself that he saw in his members another law warring against the law of his mind. The law of the Christian mind has explicitly accepted the truth that the one only God is the Creator who in Christ was

129

made man and that the manhood of Christ was full and perfect. But there is and always has been in Christendom another law warring against this law of the Christian mind, and bent on denying it as effectively as possible. For we can sincerely accept a truth with part of what we are and unknowingly reject it with another part.

Christians, for instance, believe in God's love. But if they believed in it fully with the totality of their being, they would be perfect. What keeps them sinners is that important aspects of them are incapable of thus believing and must therefore look for security elsewhere. That is why doctrinal orthodoxy by no means goes hand in hand with personal sanctity.

It follows, therefore, that without the slightest degree of conscious hypocrisy we may believe in the God of love as the Creator of all things while at the same time we may regard this Creator as a powerfully sinister force of which it behoves us to be extremely cautious, if not downright afraid, not in this instance as a savage judge with power to condemn and punish, but as the fount of vitality, as the source of impulses and instincts within us which, we fear, will sweep us off our feet. The Creator, in fact, so runs our frightened fantasy, works not for our good but for our destruction. And thus we seek protection from Him in what we may describe to ourselves as the safe arms of Christ, whose Holy Spirit will enable us to fight and conquer our enemy. It matters not that this dualistic view has been condemned from early days by the Church. For we ourselves condemn it as a matter of doctrine. With our mind we serve the law of God. But there are very few of us in whom, somewhere or other, there does not lurk a disciple of Marcion. For, however we phrase our

130

prayers, they are often in substance a cry to the Redeemer for deliverance from the Creator. Consider, for instance, the constantly recurring prayer for purity of heart. It is true that as used by Jesus the phrase meant singleness of purpose, the integration in which every aspect of the personality contributes its due share to the whole. But when most Christians pray for purity of heart they are asking for freedom from a certain type of instinctive drive. That is why, for example, in many popular manuals of devotion one of the prayers to be said at night includes the petition that from the sons of light there may be banished the deeds of darkness. There is, Heaven knows, excuse enough for such a view for those who take seriously certain passages of the New Testament. No unindoctrinated person can read St Paul's First Epistle to the Corinthians without concluding that he believed bodily desires to be inherently evil. It is no good answering that St Paul, as a Jew, could not have believed this, or that certain other passages in his writings indicate a contrary opinion. No doubt with his mind St Paul believed man's physical nature to be in itself good because God had created it. But the other law in his members warring against the law of his mind was determined to keep the Creator at as safe a distance as possible.

The same determination can be seen in the exhortations to exterminate self with which preachers often favour us. Self, we are told, is the enemy. We must choose between self and God. Now it is gloriously true that in the garden secretly and on the cross on high Christ taught His brethren and inspired to suffer and to die. But such self-sacrifice and self-surrender is possible only when selfhood has been achieved. And it is in fact an affirmation of the self, not a denial of it.

131

We do not abdicate what we are when we give ourselves away, as though we displaced ourselves in order
that God might reign where we once reigned. The
alternative between God and the self here is false. If
God is our Creator then it is by means of our being
ourselves to the fullest possible extent that He reigns.
For God is not our rival. He is the ground of our being.
And only when we begin to reign with Him in the full
possession of our human selfhood can we begin also
to suffer with Him and to die. If God is represented as
an insecure tyrant fanatically certain that the only way
to maintain his own rights is to deny all rights to his
subjects, then to serve Him becomes a form of suicide.
This is felt by a great number of people, even if most
of them could not state explicitly what is putting them
off. They smell extermination in Church, Christianity
being summarized for them in the great Command-
ment, 'You must on no account be you. That is wicked.
You must be what *we* tell you, for that is God's Word
and Law.'

A further way in which we deny the Creator and
refuse to give Him honour is in our assumption of our
own unworthiness. I know that in the language of strict
theological definition there are various degrees in which
that assumption is held. As the old joke has it, some are
only miserable sinners while others are totally depraved.
But behind such niceties of distinction, there lies a
common distrust of what God has made. It is true of
course that we have no power of ourselves to help ourselves, for we have no power of ourselves to be at all.
But the idea that we somehow do God honour by the
constant denigration of ourselves is as absurd as the
idea that the way to compliment a parent is to tell him
how horrible his children are. Behind such confessions

132

there lies, hidden and unseen, a vote of no confidence in the Creator. From this point of view one of the most significant theological books written during this century was Professor Nygren's *Agape and Eros*. For here the cat was let out of the bag. 'The man whom God loves,' wrote Professor Nygren, 'has not any value in himself. His value consists simply in the fact that God loves him'. Man somehow finds himself created, and as such in himself he has no value. God's love redeems him by giving him a value he could not acquire from an apparently worthless Creator.

This fear of the Creator and distrust of His work is a practical denial of the first of the beliefs we are considering. But it leads inevitably to a similar denial of the second. For its result, in Christian character, is a sort of monophysite piety where grace, far from perfecting nature, is called in to inhibit and suppress it. Joseph Conrad describes one of his characters as prayerfully divesting himself of the last vestiges of his humanity. The cook on board the *Narcissus* was doubtless an extreme case, but is there not an element of such a divesting in a great deal of our devotional life and practice? Those who guide us in these things tell us of rules of prayer and meditation and the like, and such practices should bring us closer to reality, and not remove us further away from it. But does this in fact happen? Very often pious practices of this kind breed a certain type of artificiality which creates a barrier between the practitioner and ordinary people. They sense the presence of something unnatural. That is why the adoption by the Church of England of theological seminaries for the training of ordinands was by no means an unmixed blessing. Too much grace and too little nature produces undertones in which there can be detected something either anaemic or hysterical. This is most emphatically not due to our theological colleges being badly or unimaginatively run. It is due to something which is spread much more widely and goes much deeper. It is due to the belief of most Christian people, a belief of which many of them are largely unaware, that if they are to serve God and show forth His goodness, then they must be a great deal less than their full selves. St Jerome's dream in which he accused himself of being a Ciceronean not a Christian is symptomatic of an important tendency in Christian feeling which still continues. It is found again in the epistle chosen by the Western Church for Easter Sunday, in which on this supreme festival of abundant life we are told to mortify our members which are upon the earth. It is not without interest that Von Hügel was quick to notice in people such self-contraction in the supposed interests of holiness, most winsomely perhaps in his estimate of Newman : 'I used to wonder, in my intercourse with John Henry Newman, how one so good, and who had made so many sacrifices to God, could be so depressing.'

But, you will be thinking, all this talk about disguised dualism and of distrusting the Creator and the human nature He has made, leaves out of account the doctrine of the Fall and of Original Sin. Well, of course, it was easier when Christians believed that God created the world as it is now in six days and that the goodness of the creation was spoilt by man's deliberate choice of evil rather than good, so that a moral disorder was handed on to all subsequent generations. Believing that, you could make a good case for distrusting natural instincts and affections, since, although they may have been originally implanted by God, they were then twisted and spoilt by human wickedness. But we know

now that this is not the manner in which the world has come to be what it is and that God moves in ways infinitely more mysterious. It looks as though an unmeasurable amount of what we can only describe as utter ruthlessness went to the making of the human race. And it would seem that in some sense the process has to be continued in the individual if he is to reach the maturity for which God intends him. When such self-assertiveness is, for this or that reason, repressed and forbidden expression, the result is a warping and distortion of the personality which brings the maximum amount of harm to itself and everybody else with whom it has to do. I suppose the most notable example of such distortion in our day was Adolf Hitler. A self-assertion he had been unable to articulate burst out in his seizure of political power and his bid to dominate the world. The point I am making was well put by Dr C. E. Raven in his Gifford Lectures, and Dr Raven is by no means credulous in matters generally described as psychological. He spoke of a phase of growth in the human individual which demands isolation of the self from the herd, the fostering of egoism, and in some measure at least the temptation to the primal sin of pride. Only so, concluded Dr Raven, can the individual acquire a self. In my own phraseology I would say that it is only by the courage to receive our natural potentialities without let or hindrance that we can become fully ourselves and that this courage to receive must, at one or more stages of our growth, involve a certain ruthless assertiveness.

This admittedly raises problems for Christology which were certainly not discussed in the fourth and fifth centuries and have seldom been raised in recent times. The New Testament is unanimous in its witness to the sinlessness of Christ, and all traditions of the Church no less. Yet the Jesus of the Synoptic Gospels (unlike the Jesus of much Christian imagination), does not give the impression of being an innocent. 'How is it that ye sought me? Wist ye not that I must be about my Father's business?' sounds ruthless but is doubtless legendary. Yet it has its counterpart in sayings generally accepted as historical. 'Who is my mother?' may be a comforting text to Protestant controversialists, but in the circumstances in which it was spoken it must have seemed what in anybody else we should not hesitate to call harsh. Even more so the damning of Judas Iscariot: 'good were it for that man if he had never been born.' That is the language of divine omniscience. In a man it would have been an infantile fantasy of omnipotence, inevitable perhaps in a human being facing final catastrophe through a friend turned traitor. Maybe our Christology must of necessity be more monophysite than we realize or are prepared to acknowledge. In spite of our intricate theologizing, it may be that in practice we are forced to live in the atmosphere of the carol, 'The cattle are lowing the baby awakes, But the little Lord Jesus no crying He makes.'

Be this as it may, and this fundamental Christological problem apart, it looks as though for mankind in general it is true that we must sin that grace may abound. It is disappointing that beyond a mere denial St Paul never answered the objection. But perhaps there is no answer, beyond the fact that the Creator and Redeemer are one, and that we must wait until we see the final result of his work before we can understand how it was achieved. Yet from another point of view this final result is something we have already seen. For when we read of the Crucified that at the hour of His death

He said, '*Consummatum est*,' what else are we being told than that God saw everything that He had made, and, behold, it was very good? Certainly those whom we feel live closest to God give the impression of being able to see Him in places where He is apparently most neglected or denied. What they seem most aware of is the capacity of the divine Compassion to meet human need, and that is because they have known themselves in desperate need of the same Compassion – perhaps in their case because they once confused the Church of God with what could be described as the Ninety and Nine Club – a confusion not uncommon among Anglicans. Perhaps we might say that those living closest to God have the assurance of things hoped for, the conviction of things not seen, and are thus capable of finding in what crucifies Christ the means whereby He is glorified and God is glorified in Him. Westcott's famous plea that the dead Christ should be removed from our crosses in favour of a Christ in majesty is not only a demand for a revision in our doctrine of Christ's death. It is an estimate of the entire human situation. If true, then the *Felix Culpa* of Holy Saturday is the highest praise we can offer to the mystery of the God-head: *O felix culpa, quae talem ac tantum meruit habere redemptorem!* O happy fault, which merited a redemption so great and of such a kind!

137

Redemption

What Christians mean by redemption is a reality so rich and many sided that it is impossible to do justice to more than an infinitesimal part of the whole. What I have to say this morning will therefore inevitably be partial and one-sided. I am not using those adjectives in the pejorative sense usually ascribed to them – a deliberate shutting of the eyes to aspects of a question which do not suit one's own convenience. What I mean is that I shall not be giving a survey of what redemption has meant in the history of Christian thought, as though this were the first draft of a Ph.D thesis. Such surveys are important and indeed essential. But they have been done. In my view, strict academic scholarship has already given to theological thinking all that for the time being it has to give. Texts have been established and their ideas elucidated. The historical method has yielded an abundant harvest. But by now all has been gathered in. And our present task is of a different kind. Like St Paul or St Augustine or Luther or St John of the Cross we must examine and try to communicate the depths of our own experience. We must discover and try to tell how God's redemption of us has made itself known to the most secret places of our being. The result will be partial and one-sided. But for all its limitations, our vision will be genuine. It will be a true expression of what we really believe instead of a mere intellectual assent to an official orthodox line. The difference between these two is emphasized in the Epistle of St James: 'Thou believest that there is one God; thou doest well: the devils also believe.' If God is infinite and incomprehensible, our apprehension of Him must inevitably be one-sided. That is a fact we must accept, not a danger we must avoid, for we cannot avoid it. No camera has yet been invented which will take the entire universe in a single shot. When people emphasize what they call the danger of one-sidedness as inseparable from the introspection and subjectivity which I have claimed is our theological task today, I believe that the danger they feel is different from what they think it is. It is danger, certainly, but not the danger they imagine. One-sidedness is what they think they fear. But in fact, as we have seen, that is inevitable whatever our method of procedure. The most traditional survey of a doctrine by the most impartial scholar is one-sided at least in the sense that what he has to offer us is entirely in the brain. It ignores a great deal of what we are. It ministers only to that part of us which is able to put two and two together, as though love were no more than a species of mathematics. No, the danger of what is called introspection or subjectivism is that it threatens our alleged autonomy. It destroys the illusion that I am in command of myself by asking, what is the I which is supposed to be in command, and what is the self which is supposed to be commanded? And the real danger is that I shall discover that my being is not in fact at all identical with my mental picture of it. To look within ourselves will thus involve us in a surrender of our imagined identity to a fuller version of what we are. And this prospect makes us frightened enough to think up good reasons for avoiding it. Hence the use of phrases like one-sided or subjective as synonymous with undesirable or mistaken.

Yet what is longed-for and needed by the world Christ came to redeem is precisely this fullness of our human nature. If the world does not listen to our gospel as much as it should, that is because people feel in their bones, even if they cannot express it clearly in their minds, that the practice of religion de-humanizes. The universal appeal of Pope John was the fullness of his humanity, and it surprised everybody, including Roman Catholics, that such humanity was to be found in the most eminent of ecclesiastics. When Pope John died, a Roman Catholic writer (Morris West) in *Life Magazine* said he hoped John would not be canonized as that would make him appear less human than in fact he was – a statement which let the cat out of the bag with a vengeance. Intellectually, as a matter of doctrine, we all assent to the opinion that grace does not destroy nature but perfects it, just as we agree as a matter of doctrine that Our Lord's humanity was complete. But that to which we thus give intellectual acceptance does not seem always to have percolated very far within ourselves. We don't always feel and behave and live as though it were true. The intellectual acceptance seems often to be a mask which disguises a more fundamental rejection.

I want therefore this morning to consider redemption in terms of our becoming full human beings. To be redeemed, in my view, is to be made whole. It is not concerned with shadowy (and indeed sometimes shady) transactions between unreal celestial figures, even when we call them the Father and the Son. In the words of John Oman, 'For mapping out from above God's operations, it must be admitted that we occupy no vantage ground. We are not able at all to soar, and we look up with no eagle eye. Only if we can see grace as it works on earth and understand it as it effects our own experience, can we possibly hope to have either clearness or certainty.' That is why I propose to consider redemption in terms of human wholeness. To be redeemed is to be richly and satisfyingly myself. Of course, each of us is both redeemed and unredeemed at the same time. At certain times and in certain ways I can be rewardingly my full self. At other times and in other ways I cannot. The mark of the unredeemed man is the craving for things to compensate him for not being fully what he is. Anything can be used as a compensatory substitute of this kind – the accumulation of riches, work, sex, alcohol, motor-racing, politics, the practice of religion. In themselves all such things are neutral in the sense that they can be *either* a genuine expression of what I really am *or* an attempt to forget the pain of not being fully myself. Most things we engage in are probably a mixture of both – partly the water of life and partly a pain-deadening drug.

But at this point we must notice a fundamental contradiction within all of us. On the one hand we long for wholeness, and in so far as we do not possess it we are in a despair which, because it is too painful to recognize, we hide from ourselves by our compensatory activities. But, on the other hand, we are afraid of the very wholeness for which we long, and fight against its growth in us. That is the tragic dichotomy in which man is involved. He longs for that against which he fights. At all costs he wants what he is determined to reject. We talk of people as the slaves of money or class or drink or sex or religion. But that is the less important part

141

of the truth. The deadly attraction of these compensatory substitutes is not so much in themselves but in the protection they give from the desire and pursuit of the wholeness of which men are terrified. Concentrate, for instance, on making money, and maybe you can stifle the fundamental but threatening desire for wholeness, or concentrate, again, on absolute orthodoxy in matters of faith and morals, and maybe you will be able to deafen yourself to your desire to accept God's invitation to heal within you what is sick and to raise up what is dead.

To want to be fully alive, to be fully without let or hindrance what I have it in me to be, such desire requires no explanation. It seems natural to us, and so, self-evident. If I have a good voice, my desire to use it in singing does not need to be explained. But the fear of wholeness and the fight against it, that does require explanation. Until we have apprehended the dynamics of this dread, we shall remain a house divided against itself. Why, then, are we frightened of wholeness? The answer is that the more whole we are, the more capable are we of suffering. If I were deaf, I would not suffer from a road-drill outside my window. If I were blind and without any sense of smell I could live contentedly in a gas-works. So far the point is obvious enough. But we are more than our physical senses. We are made up also of feelings which are deep, mysterious, and extremely vulnerable. Such feelings may be considered by us as too destructive to continue. I say 'considered by us,' but it need not be a matter of conscious decision or deliberate choice. If, for instance, the sight of blood produces within me an intolerable anxiety, a feeling too painful to be borne, then I faint. For the moment I am willing to surrender consciousness itself rather than endure the fear and stress which the sight of blood evokes. Now all of us have put certain elements of ourselves into permanent unconsciousness. According to those who have observed these things clinically, the infant and small child instinctively drive certain strong feelings into unconsciousness because such feelings are considered too destructive to have. Every human being is unique and therefore what is thus made unconscious differs in content and degree from person to person. But such an unconsciousing is universal. To an infant, its mother is its universe and its god. The infant depends entirely upon its mother for everything. To the infant (as with everybody always) to defy its universe brings destruction. Hence the infant and small child must be, not itself, but what mother wants. Such conformity is felt to be the *sine qua non* of continued existence. If, to take only one example, my mother does not give me the physical tenderness and cuddling for which I crave, then in time, and to the degree in which it is withheld, I drive my longing for physical tenderness into unconsciousness. The infant is no longer its full self. It is its full self *minus* its desire for cuddling. Or to take another example, the infant when something is withheld from it may get into a rage. When parental training takes the form of ostracizing the infant when it is in a rage, then the price is too great. Thus to destroy one's universe is to destroy oneself. So the feeling of anger is driven into unconsciousness. The infant, again, is no longer its full self, but is full self *minus* its capacity for feeling angry. In both these examples, wholeness is felt to involve destruction and disaster. And wholeness thus comes to be dreaded as lethal. Let us take another example, starting this time with a grown-up person. Why is John Smith so wet, incapable of making any decisions, or taking any initiative, just drifting with every tide? Or, to put the identical question in reverse, why is John Smith so over-assertive, always laying down the law and telling everybody what to do? Because the atmosphere in which he was brought up was hostile to his having a mind and will of his own. His parents did not want him to be John Smith, but their son, thinking, feeling and doing what they wanted. Hence he buried his capacity to make decisions and so forth, buried it deep and out of sight within himself. Otherwise, in all sorts of subtle ways, his parents would have disowned him. It was too dangerous to be himself. Hence now he either can't make decisions or is compensating for this inherent incapacity by laying down the law about everything. Here again, wholeness spelt disaster.

It is, I believe, for reasons of this kind that we are terrified of, and stubbornly resist, the very wholeness for which we also long. This terrible contradiction within our nature is not our fault – just as a man can't be blamed for fainting when he sees blood. It is not our fault. But it is our tragic predicament, common both to the priest and the people to whom he ministers. How then does Christ redeem us? How does He make us whole?

Christ, our Creator, redeems us first by His wrath. The wrath of God is His refusal to allow us to rest until we have become fully what we are. Discontent, unhappiness, suffering, are the common experience of all. Sometimes we feel them acutely. More often we are able to smother them. They hover in the wings of our personality because we don't like to see them strutting upon the stage. There are moments when they force themselves in front of the footlights and we have to take notice of them, whether we like it or not. I suspect, for example, that the heat engendered by *Honest to God* was to a large extent due to its forcing us to notice our own incompleteness. That in turn was due to our having misused traditional orthodoxy, not as a means of being confronted with the living God, but as a conspiracy to conceal from ourselves the pain of being only half of what we are. Be this as it may, unrest, doubt, the sense of apparent futility or staleness or ineffectiveness or drabness, or the sharper deeper wounds which everybody now and then must endure – these are God in His wrath, not punishing us, but refusing to let sleeping dogs lie, insisting that we be not less than we have it in us to be.

In other words Christ comes to us by means of our ordinary, common experience of living. In the heartache, the fever, and the fret, there is Christ in His wrath refusing to allow us to stay as we are, reminding us of our intolerable halfness. Whatever they believe or don't believe when people come to us in deep personal distress, what they are complaining of is one stage or element of Christ's redemptive work within them. Let us have ears to hear what these people are really telling us : that they are starting to realize that they can't go on living without receiving the wholeness of which they are terrified. I should say that all of us suffer from some degree or other of neurotic stress. It can be there, without in any way incapacitating us from doing our work. It can show itself as no more than the twitch of the finger or the mouth. The analogy with physical disease misleads us. Our neurosis is a protest against our being half-people. It may be triggered off by external circumstances, but its real cause is that a would-be-stifled part of us is insisting upon recognition, and the

status quo within is fighting back. The result is painful
to bear. But it is a sign that the work of redemption is
going on inside us. It is God's wrath against the me
that is a pharisee in order that this me may open itself
to accept and welcome the me that is a publican. Here
I hope it is obvious that the wrath of God is completely
identical with His love. It is not another aspect of God,
but one and the same thing. God's love for me the
publican is His wrath for me the pharisee who tries to
exclude the publican.

As I said, God's wrath upsets the *status quo* inside
me by refusing to allow my sleeping dogs to lie. This
is the first movement towards that redemption which
is being made whole. I suppose the apocalyptic chapters
in the Gospels can be interpreted in this light – when
travail begins and gets really severe, then look up and
lift up your heads for your redemption draweth nigh.
This upsetting of the *status quo* brings, of course, not
so much disharmony itself (since that has always been
there latently asleep) but a realization, an awareness of
the disharmony. It is necessary for us thus to be made
aware of what is within us, but disharmony cannot be
the final end. How does the ultimate harmony come
about? – I say, 'come about', and not 'recovered', because we can't recover something we never had.

The harmony comes about by the attractive and
creative power of God's love. I am no biologist, but I
imagine that a seed sown in the ground first disintegrates
(what Jesus called 'dies') and is then brought to a new
and fruitful harmony by the sun and rain. So God's
love first tears us apart in order to recreate us into a
fuller, richer being. It is in so far as this recreation has
occurred within us that we are able to perceive God's
apparently disintegrating wrath as in fact His

integrating love, not, so to speak, as a pious opinion, but as a living reality.

God's love harmonizes us by convincing us that we are accepted as a whole. To take a parallel from social life – what society accepts is the front we put on towards it – the patient voice on the telephone. When we have put the receiver down we mutter, 'Damn that woman for an infernal nuisance.' God accepts both sides of us, not just the man humbly praying on his knees, but also the man in a flaming temper. When the man in a flaming temper realizes that he is accepted, his temper ceases to have so complete a hold on him. He can laugh at himself for being that sort of man, just as we do at a man in a temper on the stage.

God's love, I said, brings us to harmony by giving us the ability, the nerve if you wish, to accept ourselves because we know we have already been accepted. Tillich's phrase about accepting our acceptance is, I think, very telling. But here I want to stress something of immense importance. God's love is incarnated love – that's what we believe. It came to us in a man, Jesus Christ. God's love was mediated through the compelling magic of a human person. This means that today God's love will not come to us as a kind of supernatural wireless-wave. It will come to us incarnated – that is, through human people, parents, husbands, wives, children, friends, pastors, parishioners, the town or village community, writers, and so on. Our notions of God's love are very often monophysite. We expect what we call the divine charity to work in us like a sort of spiritual chemical. But it is in the community, in its various elements and degrees of intensity, that God's love is mediated to us. The great saying of Jesus, 'I was hungry and ye gave me meat; I was thirsty and ye gave me drink,' that saying works both ways. We minister to Christ when we feed the hungry even when we don't think of it in those terms at all ('when saw we Thee hungry and fed Thee?'), and conversely, when we are hungry and somebody feeds us, it is Christ supplying our need, even if the person is not aware of it and calls himself an atheist or agnostic. In all works of love which we do and in all works of love which we receive, there is God Himself creating harmony. And the work of love includes attitude – the atmosphere created by a person's outlook.

The work of God's love in redemption thus goes on through the medium of the accepting community. And it is in this sense, I believe, that the church can be described as the extension of the Incarnation; in the very practical sense that Christ's impact, that is the impact of God's love continues in the attitude and actions of men and women towards each other. Naturally I can talk only in terms of the job I have to do in Cambridge. From time to time I am amazed and deeply moved by the concern and interest and compassion and love which my young people show towards each other. And in this, I believe, God's love is in their midst. And its humanizing power is obvious. A young man or woman often arrives at the University at odds with himself or herself and the world. The accepting atmosphere into which they are received gives them the confidence to face the disharmony within. What was once anaesthetized is allowed to wake up and cause trouble. But then the work of the accepting community proceeds and creates the beginnings of a more comprehensive harmony. Of course the work has to go on afterwards, generally through marriage, family, and a responsible job. But these people are moving towards

148

the fullness of their human nature, and this is what I mean when I say they are being redeemed. As they grow older, new situations will arouse further dormant forces within them. And so again there will be trouble and tension. But again it may happen that they will be brought within the harmonizing influence of an accepting society. Their wives and friends will stand by them and communicate the divine charity.

I want to end by speaking of something which I find very hard to put into words. In so far as we live for others – I am aware of how little I myself do – but in so far as we live for others, we do so not only by our actions and attitudes (of which I have already spoken) but also by (what is inseparable from them) our interior state, what we are and what we experience most deeply inside us. The happiness and misery which come to us, the exulting and the agony, we experience as individuals alone. But they are not for us alone. They are for mankind. When we thank God in our joy or cry to Him in our pain, we articulate the prayers of the world – prayers which, for this reason or that, perhaps cannot be articulated in some hearts. So we find ourselves offering our joy or our pain to God to be used to help others. There have been periods in my life – and it must also be true of all of us here – periods of black despair when the only thing that we could do with our distress was to ask God, however half-heartedly and fitfully, to use it to bring light and peace to others. After all, Christ has called us, invited us, to share His cross. And this doesn't mean merely putting up with it. It means offering it for the salvation of souls. These are extreme moments. But we can do much the same when we are on a more even keel. Talking to people in a pub or at supper we find their most hidden desires for goodness

149

and love revealed beneath the surface of what they say. It may simply be a chance remark or an immediately forgotten exclamation. But they show what the person is feeling after, and in our own hearts, as we continue the conversation, we can seize upon this desire of theirs (hidden to a large extent even from themselves) and articulate it in a silent movement of our heart to God; for it is Christ in them, the hope of glory. It is a revelation of God at work redeeming. It owes nothing to our words or deeds, so the prayer is really an act of worship for God's own goodness and love thus manifested in those we are talking with. It is another way in which we are allowed to participate in the redemptive process.

As I said at the start, I don't think theology consists in juggling about with intellectual concepts, but in examining and trying to communicate our own deepest experiences. That is what St Paul was doing when, for instance, he wrote I Corinthians 13. And if, finally, you ask me by what signs we can recognize human wholeness when we see it, it is to I Corinthians 13 that I would point for the most concise and complete description. And that portrait was taken, not from dogma, but from life.

Christ the answer to twentieth-century need

No Christian would deny that Christ is greater than the theological systems in which men have attempted to expound His significance. We read of Jesus in the gospels, that surrounded once by a crowd who wanted to do Him violence, 'He passed through the midst of them and went His way'. So it is with the established Christian orthodoxies. In so far as they want to take Him by force and emprison Him within the boundaries of a particular point of view, Christ eludes them and goes His way. For He belongs everywhere and will be confined nowhere.

He belongs therefore to our contemporary age. That is not for one moment to deny that He belonged equally to past ages. For that would be to confine Him to our own. We cannot ignore the witness to Him borne by His disciples in any and every century. But men understand themselves and their world in different ways in different periods of history. St Paul said of himself that he was made all things to all men that he might by all means save some. A disciple is not greater than his lord. Christ is our redeemer now. In the middle of this twentieth-century He meets our needs as they are felt and understood by us. If the ministers of His church preach a fourth-century or a sixteenth-century, or a nineteenth-century Christ, then when people ask for bread they are given a stone. The gospel is not proclaimed. It is true that Jesus Christ is the same yesterday, today and for ever. But that means that always He is willing to take the form of a servant, ministering to us, not from a pedestal of divine invulnerability, but in terms of our own particular culture with its own special questions and its own special needs. Only so can we continue to say of Him that we have, not a high priest who cannot be touched with the feeling of our infirmities, but one who was at all points put to the test as we are.

How are we put to the test today? I would suggest that it is in two main directions, closely related to each other. The first concerns the assessment of human responsibility, individual and collective. The second has to do with the search for personal integrity, the need and the duty to discover our individual selves. Unless we can hear what Christ is saying to people in that predicament, confronted with that task, we cannot proclaim Him effectively to our world.

First, then, the assessment of responsibility. That there is something very wrong with the world nobody in his senses would deny. But how did this state of affairs come about? We can no longer believe that the universe was created perfect and that man spoilt it by his wanton wickedness. Nature was red in tooth and claw before man came on to the scene. And it was in virtue of the same utter ruthlessness that man emerged supreme over the other animals in the evolutionary process. The past history of humanity still lingers in human blood. How far can we be blamed for acting on instincts in virtue of which alone we find ourselves existing at all? That question was easier to answer in Darwin's generation than in our own. For they then believed that by whatever means man came to be a rational being he was now equipped with reason, and that it was this higher part of his nature which should control his lower instincts. For us that remains true only in part. For we often find it extremely difficult to distinguish between reason and rationalization. Our capacity to order our experience, to sort it out and evaluate it, our capacity to think, seems like a musical instrument on which a number of tunes can be called and we are not certain who it is who pays the piper. Animal herds will kill whatever appears to threaten their survival. Human societies act on the same instincts, but they give reasons for what they do. Centuries later there can still be argument among historians on the reasonableness of the reasons given. But that is irrelevant. At the time, the reasons given, reasonable or not, are generally believed in with complete sincerity by those who give them. How then are we to assess responsibility? When, for instance, churchmen burnt heretics, what moved them was the law of the jungle – the threat to the herd from those members of the species which deviated from the established patterns. But churchmen did not think of it in those terms. They thought with the deepest conviction that they were obeying the righteous will of the Most Holy God. How far then were they blameworthy? The same question-mark hangs over individuals. Within a certain limited area we are free to choose between one course of action and another. But we can never be sure of the exact nature or extent of that area. It is possible, for instance, for a man to be lazy, to choose deliberately to fritter his time away on trivialities when he could be doing something valuable. But apparent laziness is not always due – I would say it is seldom due – to a free choice of this kind. Within each of us there lies concealed an army of hidden persuaders. If we could decipher what they said, we should be free to accept or reject it. But often we cannot decipher. We do their bidding and ascribe our actions to completely different motives, not necessarily excusing ourselves, but often the opposite, accusing ourselves of sin and evil. I know a man who used to behave with extreme unkindness to his wife, and then went into agonies of remorse about his egotism and selfishness. It went on thus for five years. Then he discovered that his unkindness was prompted by a hidden persuader of which he at last became aware – the ghost within himself of a tyrannical and possessive mother whom he had to fight in order to grow up at all, and whose image he was unknowingly projecting upon the woman he had married. Could this man be blamed for his unkindness to his wife?

This doubt concerning the assessment of human responsibility is in our age combined with the sense of an inescapable imperative to seek and find what we are. Our concern here is with the relation of this imperative to possible religious attitudes, that is, attitudes towards God. I believe that there can be – and generally is – serious conflict at this point. I also believe that the conflict is unnecessary and is due chiefly to a misunderstanding of the meaning of worship.

Perhaps we can proceed thus: before God in His infinite goodness and surpreme value, it looks as though a man should feel very small, unworthy, wretched, if not completely valueless. The language of devotion is full of phrases expressing attitudes of this kind. We need go no further than the words of the well-known hymn, 'Just as I am without one plea'. Such an attitude towards God is held to be an indispensable element in

154

our love for him, the *sine qua non* of our advance in
his service. Those who instruct us in the paths of prayer
always tell us that the nearer a man approaches God
the more completely sinful he feels. If you think this is
an exclusively Protestant phenomenon, you should read
the devotional literature of the Counter-Reformation.

Yet worship surely is concerned exclusively with the
simple but profound matter of response to perceived
value. We experience it in daily life when we are confronted with something of overwhelming beauty or some
act of sublime heroism. If such earthly things call forth
our worship, then *a fortiori* it is meet and right that we
should worship the source from which they spring. But
such worship is concerned with the value of the object
worshipped, and in so worshipping we forget ourselves.
When attention is diverted from God to us, from his
worshipfulness to our wretchedness, then to call our
activity worship is a rationalization. In spite of our
sincerity, what we are doing is not above board. We are
not in fact responding to God's infinite value. We are
surreptitiously doing something else. What is this something else? I believe we are acting upon an unobserved
instinctive fear : the fear of standing on our own feet,
natural enough in a small child, but in an adult nothing
but a suit of armour to protect him from God's creative
power. The armour is forged by means of the following
monologue : 'You have all value in yourself. I don't
want to have any value in myself. For if you have it all
and I have none, then I can remain in childish dependence upon you. I needn't grow. So long as I feel
a worthless creature in your almighty hands, I can avoid
the quest for personal integrity.' It was because he
thought that the practice of religion was inextricably
bound up with this pseudo-worship that Freud rejected

religion as the enemy of moral development. He was right in so far as many Christians indulge in this pseudo-worship. He was wrong in his confusion of pseudo-worship with real worship, of the genuine response to value with the evasion of our moral responsibility to seek and find ourselves. The age in which we live is intensely aware of the duty to seek and find the self. Its suspicion of authority, its criticism of established criteria, its art forms, all are a response to what is felt to be life's major moral challenge – how to discover and be what I am. In these circumstances to preach Christ as he who demands unqualified submission to another, human or divine, is to confront the world not with Christ but with Judas Iscariot. Hence the feeling of fresh air and freedom when a perfectly orthodox element of Christian belief is pointed out and emphasized – that God is not an object in the universe of objects, that indeed He does not appear in the picture at all since He is the canvas on which it is painted. Of course, what I have described as life's major moral challenge can and must, in religious language, be called the will of God. But to respond to that challenge is not to submit to an external authority. It is to discover from within what we are. This distinction is not new, but it is crucial, since few things bedevil the Christian religion so much as this ambiguity in the notion of obedience. A small child will obey his father's commands. But this is altogether different from admiring your father and discovering you have it in you to be like him. The first is the spirit of bondage unto fear. The second is that glorious liberty which we believe is God's will for us.

It will be seen how both the uncertainty about blameworthiness, and the deep sense of an inescapable imperative to seek what we are until we find it – that

156

these two aspects of our contemporary culture make a sixteenth- or a nineteenth-century Christ powerless to redeem the men and women of our age. For among Christians of those former times it was taken as axiomatic that where there was evil, man was to blame if not individually then collectively, and that his fundamental sin was precisely his quest for personal integrity, his eating of the fruit of the tree of knowledge in defiance of the divine authority which had forbidden him to do so. Thus you admitted you were blameworthy, confessed your sin of disobedience, believing that if it were a matter of strict justice there was no future for you outside hell. But God would forgive you and restore you the blessings you had justly forfeited. Indeed, God had forgiven you already by sending his Son into the world to die. Christ on the cross shows us how blameworthy we are, how utterly inexcusable was our disobedience to authority, but assures us none the less that if we confess our sin and admit our guilt we shall be received and pardoned.

It is not pride which prevents people today from accepting this account of our redemption. It is honesty – a refusal to ignore facts about the past history of the human race and the functioning of the human psyche – what we find without us and within. As honesty generally does, it brings with it here its own particular pain. For the unquestioning acceptance of our own blameworthiness, leading to confession and pardon, possessed, for those who had experience of it, something of the warmth and comfort of the nursery? But our age has been sent away to school. Once again we have eaten of the fruit of the tree of knowledge and things can never be the same. Yet it is not for ministers of Christ's word to cling nostalgically to the warmth and pleasures of a past now dead. Christ is the Saviour of men and women today, people who certainly are looking for salvation but who cannot look for it except in terms of their own predicament and cannot find it in anything which would betray what they feel most deeply to be their main task and duty as human beings.

What has Christ to give to such people, to give to us? What is the character of that life of which He said that He had come that men might have it more abundantly? We cannot think of it in terms of some spiritual essence or celestial power, for as thus considered it is meaningless. Must we not rather search the Scriptures, believing that the word of God therein set forth will be made flesh in our own day and generation? This is not the search for historical objectivity – for what really happened, or for what was really said. That search has been tried and has failed. It is rather faith that the Bible can speak God's word to us now and that that word will incarnate itself in terms of our own contemporary needs, taking as always the form of a servant. When, in this faith, we study the gospels, what do we find?

We find a Christ who was not a saint as that term is commonly and mistakenly understood. We find a Christ who did not always do the ideal thing. We discover that the notion that He did is wishful thinking – a refusal to accept the full fact of His humanity. For in human life, it is generally not possible to do the ideal thing. The claims men have to meet very often clash with each other, so that you cannot give to every claim what is its due. So, for instance, Jesus gave Himself to His work at the expense of His family to whom He appears to have been brutal. And Jewish scholars of great integrity have noticed that Jesus was so concerned to proclaim His own message that He was sometimes unfair to His opponents. In the circumstances of human life that sort of one-sidedness is inevitable. And Jesus was not magically preserved from the contradictions, the conflicting claims which are the inevitable lot of men. But in one thing He was absolutely consistent. The truth He proclaimed, the truth by which He lived, the truth for which He died, was his own. He discovered it for Himself within Himself. He did not buy it ready-made from its professional purveyors. On that point He never compromised. That is why the people heard Him with astonishment and recognized that He taught with authority and not as the scribes. He spoke, that is, from His own first-hand experience and not from an acquired knowledge of other people's ideas. He did not mould His person or His ministry to any pre-conceived notion. He carefully avoided the application to Himself of any title which might suggest such pre-conceptions. If He applied passages of the Old Testament to Himself, we do not know which ones He selected. Was it Isaiah? Was it Daniel? Was it both? Was it neither? This uncompromising loyalty to His own identity, to the truth which was Himself, brought Him power and joy. The crowds listened in wonder while He spoke of ordinary things in common experience – a farmer sowing or reaping, a woman baking bread, an animal which had strayed – and opened up these things, like the poet He was, to tell of secrets greater than themselves. But He had also to pay the price which must always be paid by those who have the courage to receive their own vision instead of accepting the available stereotypes – isolation, loneliness, the ultimate opposition of the crowds He formerly attracted, absolute hostility from the appointed guardians of faith and morals. Yet the

159

most costly of the sacrifices He had to make in order to receive and hold to His own identity was the loss of His confidence. Perhaps from the start He had been the victim of an illusion. After all, that sort of thing had occurred fairly frequently in the history of His people. They had always had their false prophets as well as their true ones. And many of the false prophets had been sincere enough according to their lights. They had just been a bit mad, that was all. Had He been a bit mad too? And was the defection of Judas the moment of disillusioning sanity? Had He sacrificed everything to a fanatic's dream? After all, His relatives had thought Him mad, and had once tried to force him home. Such torturing doubts must come to any man who refuses to play safe, to accept what he is told, and can they fail to have been part of Christ's agony and bloody sweat, seeing that He died with the most dreadful of all questions upon His lips, 'My God, why hast thou forsaken me?' So, might ask a cynic or a fighter for orthodoxy, so, is that where the search for personal integrity led Him and left Him? Perhaps He should be a warning to us all instead of a Saviour. Yet many today can identify themselves with Him in His search and in His doubt. They are somehow aware that what He did and suffered gives meaning to what they have set themselves to do and are prepared to suffer. And it gives this meaning to their experience not in spite of His death in despair but because of it. To hold to one's own vision, to be loyal to what one has discovered for oneself within oneself up to the point of dying apparently forsaken by God and man – this, we sense, is life and life abundant. Were not the first disciples of Jesus brought to the same conclusion? They saw Him die and heard His cry of despair. Yet they proclaimed Him

160

Lord and bore witness to Him that He was alive for evermore. The last of the evangelists wrote of His death as an act of triumphant majesty in which He was exalted and glorified. Whatever is meant by the resurrection of Christ, it did not alter what had happened on the cross, nor did it, at the thirteenth hour, save a situation which had got out of hand. The resurrection rather, as Westcott said, 'was the passage to the proper realm of truth – of that which really *is*'. And the death of Jesus was now seen in that light of truth for what it really was : not a tragedy but a victory, not the worst evil but the best good, not suffering but glory, not death but life. To quote Westcott again, 'We have that to make known which cannot be measured or tested by limited standards : that which justifies itself simply by shining.' When in our own bewilderment and doubt we are condemned by the orthodoxies and begin to believe them when they tell us God has forsaken us, when thus we come to know the fellowship of Christ's sufferings, that is the precise point where we also know the power of His resurrection. And that is what redemption means.

Nor do we have to engage on the fruitless and impossible task of assessing responsibility. No doubt sometimes we are to blame, but we can accept our uncertainty about how much and when. For, in the light of the resurrection, what is important about Christ's death is not the assessment of Judas's or Caiaphas's or Pilate's responsibility, but the death itself as revealing Christ's glory and drawing all men unto Him. From the point of view of Christian faith, so completely does God make all things into the instruments of goodness that we are driven to say that had there been no Judas, no Caiaphas and no Pilate the

161

loss to humanity would have been irreparable. That at least was the view of St Paul as expounded in the ninth to the eleventh chapters of the Epistle to the Romans. Speaking of his own people, the Jews, he said that, because they offended, salvation had come to the Gentiles, and that their offence meant the enrichment of the world. This conversion of all things to the service of goodness is again what redemption means. And this redemption is what the Church affirms at the centre of its greatest act of worship. In the recitation of the *Agnus Dei,* all thought of blame, all attempts to assess responsibility, are cast aside in the presence of what God has done and is doing – 'O Lamb of God which taketh away the sin of the world.' That is the joy of the everlasting gospel and the joy is the worship.

The Saints

Do you know, or have you ever known, a saint? Of course, one or two of the people we meet very occasionally for the odd half-hour we might perhaps describe as a saint. Father Theophilus, for instance, of Soulfield: he always looks extremely holy and was wonderful when he took tea with me three years ago and talked so naturally about prayer. Or Sister Juliana: do you remember when she showed us round the convent with her quiet dignity and serene composure? Or that man who works among the down-and-outs in Naples – or is it Paris? His achievements speak for themselves, and when I heard him talk at that meeting in London I could feel God's power at work in the Hall.

These are imaginary characters, but we must all have come across people like them. Nobody denies that they are servants of the Lord – and profitable servants. But in fact we know very little indeed about them. The blanks are much larger than the bits we can draw, and these blanks we fill in from our own imagination, projecting on to them our own ideas of saintliness. If we knew more of Father Theophilus and Sister Juliana and the man in Paris, had to work with them and share with them a small house with only one common sitting-room and one common bathroom, we might begin to have reservations about their sanctity – 'Yes, he is a saint, *in a way*. But you know he can be rather selfish about the bathroom. He is ruining his lungs with that filthy pipe-tobacco. I don't mind, but he really should sometimes think of Sister Juliana. And he may do wonderful work, but, my goodness, it has to be done exactly the way he wants it or else the balloon goes up. He's really an egotist.'

But on All Saints Day we should be thinking of real people, not cardboard characters. All right, let's do it properly and go to the very top of the list. Not for us Saint Canute, king and martyr, or Saint Hyacinth, confessor. Let us choose people no less than St Peter and St Paul – about whom we have a good deal of information and who were both (let us say at once) put to death for their faith. First, St Peter. Preachers often exhort us to consider the difference between St Peter before the resurrection of Our Lord and after. And indeed it is true that whereas he once ran away from death, in the end, for Christ's sake, he was ready to endure it. But that isn't the whole story. Peter's weakness of will, his inability to endure a disapproving atmosphere, shown first in the hall of the high priest when he denied Our Lord, appears again some twenty years after the resurrection. At Antioch he took meals with Gentile Christians, disregarding the Jewish food laws, and no doubt he was extremely happy in that atmosphere of brotherly approval. Then there arrived at Antioch some Jewish Christians from Jerusalem who, in characteristically religious fashion, were shocked and disgusted at Peter's disregard of the Jewish Law. And what did Peter do? Hold fast to his principles regardless of Jerusalems' disapproval? Not at all. He drew back from the Gentile Christians and discontinued eating with them, denying the truth as he clearly saw it. At that point St Paul arrived back at Antioch and didn't mince his words. 'I opposed Peter to the face,' writes Paul, 'because he stood condemned.' And there let us

164

leave Peter, caught between the Jewish Christians from Jerusalem on the one side and the apostle of the Gentiles on the other. It couldn't have been a very pleasant experience.

And what of St Paul himself? His achievements we all know. No doubt we should not now ourselves be Christians but for him. But, when in a tranquil mood, he was the first to admit that he was very far from perfect. And indeed this fact is borne out both by his letters and the Acts of the Apostles. First of all there was a quarrel with his travelling companion, Barnabas, about a young man called John Mark. We don't know the details, but we are told that the dispute with Barnabas was so acute that Paul and he parted company and went different ways. Then Paul sometimes lost his temper with his flock and indulged in orgies of self-concern. They weren't grateful enough. That was a major complaint. Particularly, they weren't grateful enough that he wasn't a financial liability to them like other apostles. 'Have I not the right to my food and drink? Have I not the right to take a wife about with me like the rest of the apostles and the Lord's brothers and Peter? Or am I alone bound to work for my living? Did you ever hear of a man serving in the army at his own expense? Yet that's what I do.' Or, even worse than this sort of ingratitude, they said he hadn't much of a presence and that as a speaker he was beneath contempt. At this Paul was furious. 'What fools,' he wrote, 'to measure themselves by themselves, to find in themselves their own standard of comparison. And, if it comes to bragging, so many people brag of their earthly distinctions that I'm going to do the same. I've suffered this, that, and the other for the gospel – prison, flogging, shipwreck – *and* fourteen years ago I had the

165

most wonderful mystical experience.'

Well, it all sounds very human and very like ourselves. These two saints at the top of the list don't seem
very saintly. But that is exactly why I have chosen
to speak of them as I have. For, in general, our views
of what a saint is like are totally unrealistic. We think
in terms of an all-round moral perfection, a man,
tempted no doubt on a grand heroic scale, but unmoved
by the pettier concerns which agitate us. When, however, you find out more about them, you discover that
this simply isn't true. They too, like us, were touchy,
quarrelsome, wanting the approval of others, sometimes
breaking their principles to get it, and capable of hitting
back hard at those who whispered uncomplimentary
things about them.

Then what are we doing celebrating All Saints Day?
Are we just indulging in excitement because we enjoy
it, once again deliciously sipping the brandy of the
damned?

But saintliness doesn't mean all-round perfection.
That is a childish dream – the sort of legend which
many English people fastened on to Queen Victoria at
the time of the Diamond Jubilee. Saintliness means one
thing only: some quality or aspect of Christ built up
in a person through the creative work of the Holy Spirit.
It may be simply one aspect of Christ and one only –
His courage, for instance – and this may be combined
with other characteristics which fall very far short of
Christ. Look at Mr Smith in the next street. He seemed
no more than an ordinary sort of chap. We tried more
than once to rope him in to some of the activities con-
nected with the church, but he always refused. He
preferred to spend his evenings watching the telly, and
his wife used to tell her more intimate women friends that

166

he was rather selfish about not going out. She wanted to meet people and he didn't. So they didn't. Of course, it was his daughter he really doted on. Then – do you remember? – both his wife and daughter were killed in a motor smash. It broke him up completely and for a time he thought he was going mad. Then he forced himself to go out and meet people. In spite of his terrible feelings of desolation, he accepted invitations to drinks and supper. He stood for the town-council and campaigned for better housing, all the time carrying that appalling load of intolerable wretchedness. It is true that for a long time we weren't aware of Christ's courage in Mr Smith, but that was because he had no need to be courageous. Then his time came, and Mr Smith, by the courage he showed, revealed to us all something of Christ. Meeting him then, seeing him going about his work, enabled us to know Christ a little better. And when, the following Holy Week, the story of Christ's agony was read out in the gospel, it seemed somehow more real for what we had seen in Mr Smith.

That is what saintliness is: something of Christ revealed in a person. It may be all sorts of things. I don't think she knows it for a moment, but Mrs Jones has the power of making people feel accepted, valued, and at home, in her company. That is a most precious quality of Christ, revealing the goodness and mercy of God and His generous love. And that again is what saintliness means, and it can be combined, on occasions, with a capacity to be extremely irritating, and not a little pushing.

But at this point let us not forget that Christ is the Creator of all things, the Eternal Word who lighteneth every man. Church people must always be aware of the temptation to make Christ into the private hero of their cosy little group. Christ the Creator, for instance, is in the scientist as he carries out experiments which lead to a new understanding of the creation. And in the satisfaction of the scientist at his discovery it is Christ who is beholding what He has made and finding it very good. Or when, in India, Ghandi practised the non-violence he preached, and thus became a power in the land, in him too something of Christ was revealed. Or, to pass from the great to the unimportant, that argumentative agnostic in the rooms above mine: when he saw I was looking miserable and invited me up to drink his gin – didn't Jesus say that on such an occasion He Himself was the guest?

But now perhaps you think I am turning the Communion of Saints into a Gilbert and Sullivan opera:

> In short, whoever you may be,
> To this conclusion you'll agree,
> When every one is somebodee,
> Then no one's anybody.

But those words of W. S. Gilbert are echoed in what the New Testament has to say about saints. They are not the spiritually aristocratic few, a sort of churchy House of Peers which appeals to the spiritual snob in each of us. All the members of Christ's Body are saints, and in the purpose of God Christ's Body includes all mankind. What we are celebrating this morning St Paul called the summing up of all things in Christ. But in the world, said Jesus, we shall have tribulation. Yet we are of good cheer because Christ has overcome the world. That, too, we are celebrating today. At All Saints Easter opens up like a fan to include everybody. We are assured that He who has begun a good work in us all will perfect it unto the day of Jesus Christ.